I0810854

2014

大成食品蛇口有限公司

2015

大成食品蛇口有限公司

2022

FOREWORD

Doreen Heng LIU

An Atypical Journey of an Industrial Heritage Site

When we talk about Shenzhen, we can never ignore its legendary transformation from fishing villages to an international metropolis within a mere 40 years. Shekou, Shenzhen, stands as the forerunner of China's Reform and Opening-up policy, which ushered in the rapid process of urbanization and economic development in the Pearl River Delta region and across the country, while Dacheng Flour Factory and other earliest foreign-funded factories in this area represent the epicenter and cornerstone of the explosive development of the city and China as a whole.

History of the Spatial Production

Built in 1980 and formerly known as Far East Flour Mills (H.K.) Limited, Dacheng Flour Factory was the first wholly foreign-owned and exclusively operated enterprise introduced by China Merchants Group to Shekou Industrial Zone. The factory was one of the Top Ten High-quality Construction Projects of Shenzhen in 1983 due to its creative application of bored piling techniques of railway bridge construction in civil engineering when its silos were constructed.

In 1990, Taiwan DaChan Food Group[1] acquired the Far East Flour Mills and established the Dachan Food (Shekou) company. The factory began to produce and promote premium flours for baking, creating brands "DaChan" for export sales and "Iron-Man" for domestic sales in Hong Kong and the Pearl River Delta region. In 2010, the factory ended its operations as a result of industrial upgrading and transformation of the area. Although the scenes of the prosperous production are gone, its buildings remain and still tell the story of their past. Due to its location at the junction of the old factory area of the 1980s of Shekou Industrial Zone and the planned new area of Prince Bay, the tensions between the old and new urban fabrics have arisen during the development process of the surrounding areas in recent years.

Experiments of Urban Regeneration

In 2005, Shenzhen Municipal Government initiated the world's first biennale dedicated exclusively to urbanism and architecture: the Bi-City Biennale of Urbanism\Architecture (UABB). Co-organized by the neighboring cities of Shenzhen and Hong Kong, the biennale uses curation as an action plan to explore the urban challenges brought about by the rapid urbanization of the Pearl River Delta region. Unlike any other biennale worldwide, UABB offers radical, forward-looking spatial experiments across different city locations, proactively addressing urban regeneration and spatial transformation in the era of urban stock.

The first UABB, themed "City, Open Door!" and curated by Yung Ho CHANG, was held within Shenzhen's OCT-LOFT area, transforming unadorned 1980s factory buildings into exhibition spaces, setting a precedent for urban regeneration in the region. The second UABB in 2007, curated by MA Qingyun and themed "City of Expiration and Regeneration," explored the life cycle of

1 — "DaChan" and "Dacheng" are different spellings for the same Chinese name "大成," while "DaChan" is used officially in the group's name, "Dacheng" is more prevalent Mandarin spelling used in Mainland China.

urban environments, bringing attention to the issues of expiration, aging, and regeneration in a timely and prescient manner. In 2013, the fifth UABB "Urban Border" was held at the Float Glass Factory in Shekou, directly tackling urban regeneration again through its venue. Ole BOUMAN, one of the curators, stated, "Through the biennale as a catalyst, we aim to make the transforming Shekou Industrial Zone generate new value."

The 2015 UABB selected Dacheng Flour Factory as the main venue. Themed "Re-living the City," the biennale was curated by Aaron BETSKY, Hubert KLUMPNER, Alfredo BRILLEMBOURG, and me. The theme responds to the rapid globalization and urbanization occurring worldwide: "We have enough physical conditions, enough houses, enough objects, enough images; as urban and architectural spaces are still expanding, they also bring irreversible disasters. What we need is to rethink, reuse and re-imagine what we already have, taking charge of the designing actions to reconstruct the cities we inhabit."

Reproduction of Space

The exhibition venue design principle proposed and implemented by me and my architectural practice NODE is to "adapt to and give full play to the existing conditions and maximize reuse of objects." Specifically, it meant to retain and strengthen the diversified original quality of this industrial heritage of distinctive features, then implant the new functions with a process of "spatial reproduction." Ultimately, The exhibition venue was created as a cultural complex, a community with a sense of utopia on this industrial heritage left from the rapid development. The renovation of Dacheng Flour Factory was a response to and an experimental project of the "Re-Living the City" strategy in itself: to reactivate, reuse and reinvent existing space.

The design and construction of the entire site was once again exemplified "Shenzhen Speed," leaving me and my team with many regrets and reflections. However, for the exhibition participants, it was an inspiring experience: design transformed from a top-down privilege for planners and architects into a collaborative process that encouraged active participation and creation. The renovated Dacheng Flour Factory appeared to be a series of scattered, random and responsive spaces and objects freely assembled, rather than an elaborate complex realized through the traditional, highly controlled method of design implementation. The final presentation of Dacheng Flour Factory was described as "uncontrollably rough and raw." However, the reproduction of diversity was a seed of hope for the future.

An Atypical Journey of an Industrial Heritage Site

Unfortunately, only six months after the exhibition, the renovated Building #8 was demolished, and a wide road leading to Prince's Bay took its place as previously planned in the blueprint. Although NODE proposed to retain it with an alternative traffic planning, it was not accepted. Later, Building #3 and the Auditorium, which was used for public events, were also demolished. Though the mill building and the iconic silos were preserved, they fell into silence amidst the ever-changing construction around them. Eight years later, the remaining parts of the Dacheng Flour Factory will be renovated again, but it is more likely to be diverted from its original purpose of being a public cultural heritage site under the strong influence of capital.

Dacheng Flour Factory, in the midst of many uncertainties, is an atypical but universal case in the rapid urbanization process of the Pearl River Delta region. We now revisit it with questions in mind, and through close observation and chronological research, we retrace its history together with the stakeholders, hoping this will lead to a reflection on the current situation of industrial heritage conservation and urban regeneration on a larger scale, with a view to promoting real change.

Doreen Heng LIU
July 2023

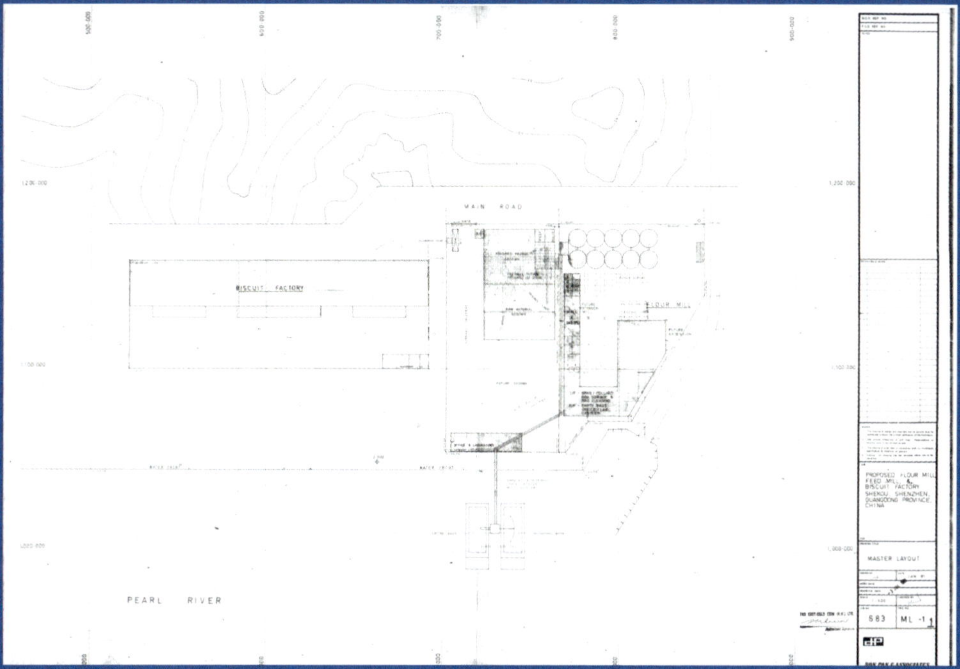

Original plan of the flour factory, 1981

Dacheng Flour Factory and surroundings in the 1990s

CONTENTS

I. HISTORY

From the perspectives of time and space

Ever since the inception of China's Reform and Opening-up in 1979, Shenzhen has embarked upon an extraordinary expedition characterized by unprecedentedly rapid urbanization. Situated in the Pearl River Delta region and in close proximity to Hong Kong, Shenzhen benefits from its advantageous geopolitical position and stands as a quintessential representation of China's impressive transformation during this critical era. Within a span of just over four decades, Shenzhen has undergone a development process that could take the Western cities a century to accomplish, and evolved into a fascinating global metropolis. With Shenzhen and the Pearl River Delta region where it is located swiftly entering the stage of stock era, this area, distinguished as one of the regions with the highest spatial density in the world, finds itself confronted by unprecedented hardships and challenges.

Serving as the vanguard of the Reform and Opening-up, Shekou Industrial Zone has experienced rapid cycles of industrial transformation and continuous upgrading driven by economic development. Dacheng Flour Factory, built during the nascent stage of the city, stands as an allegory of the era. It narrates the memories of the city and the changes it witnessed amidst the tide of urban evolution.

Location of Dacheng Flour Factory in Pearl River Delta Region

Location of Dacheng Flour Factory in Shekou, Shenzhen

Shekou Industrial Zone

Shekou area is located in the southwest corner of Shenzhen. It is near from the estuary of the Pearl River, with the northwest of the New Territories, Hong Kong across the sea. In January 1979, it was selected by China Merchants Group(CMG) and approved as an industrial zone.

In July 1979, the development of Shekou Industrial Zone started with the sole investment of CMG, making Shekou the forerunner of China's Reform and Opening-up policy. Meanwhile, the bay area in Shekou started to see the planning and construction of more factories.

"Make Shekou the most livable place for human beings."
– YUAN Geng, Founder of Shekou Industrial Zone, Shenzhen, Vice President of the board of CMG from 1979-1992

1979

1980

In August 1980, Shenzhen Special Economic Zone was established, becoming one of the four earliest economic zones in China that opened up to the outside world.

Dacheng Flour Factory

In April 1980, China Merchants Group reached an agreement with Far East Flour Mills (H.K.) Limited to establish Far East (China) Flour Mills Limited in Shekou Industrial Zone with the former company's sole ownership.

Located in the northeast corner of Prince Bay, south of Gangwan Avenue, the Flour Factory is the first wholly foreign-owned and exclusively operated enterprise introduced by CMG to Shekou Industrial Zone.

In 1981, the infrastructure construction of Shekou Industrial Zone (Phase I), including access to water, electricity, roads, navigation, communication and land leveling was completed, followed by the design and construction of a number of industrial buildings as planned.

"Time is Money, Efficiency is Life."
– YUAN Geng, Founder of Shekou Industrial Zone, Shenzhen, Vice President of the board of CMG from 1979-1992

"Shekou Industrial Zone gives full play to the autonomy of enterprises and used economic methods for construction...In less than two years, the construction of foundation works and public facilities was completed on the once barren beaches across the entire industrial zone, and the construction of a series of factories and enterprises has started. The 'Shekou Model' has drawn widespread attention."
– "Shekou Industrial Zone Witnessed Its Fast Construction Speed", a dispatch of Xinhua News Agency, published on *People's Daily*, June 17, 1981

1981

1982

In the first half of 1982, the Far East Flour Mills was completed and put into use.

The construction was undertaken by Guangzhou Branch of China Civil Engineering Construction Corporation, using integral slipforms. The factory was one of the Top Ten High-quality Construction Projects of Shenzhen in 1983 due to its innovative application of bored piling techniques, commonly used in railway bridge construction, for its silos.

1990

In October 1990, Taiwan's DaChan Great Wall Group took over Far East Flour Mills and established DaChan Food (Shekou) Co., Ltd., which started producing and promoting a range of premium baking flour, becoming well-known in the domestic and international flour industry.

"In order to enhance regional competitiveness, DaChan Group set up an aquatic product business in Indonesia, a feed factory in Shenyang, Liaoning Province and a flour factory in Shekou, Shenzhen in Guangdong Province in Chinese Mainland."
– Introduction to the History of DaChan Group

Shekou Industrial Zone

2002

In 2002, the plan concept of Prince Bay was adjusted, proposing to transform the original terminal for bulk and general cargo and containers into a terminal for international cruises and Guangdong-Hong Kong-Macao passengers, as well as a coastal commercial and business area, making it the most important maritime gateway of Shenzhen.

2006

In 2006, Urban Planning & Design Institute of Shenzhen (UPDIS) conducted the redevelopment planning of the Prince Bay Passenger Transport Hub.

2009

In 2009, the Detailed Blueprint of the Prince Bay Area was revised.

2010

In January 2010, the Urban Planning, Land and Resources Commission of Shenzhen Municipality adopted the plot ratio increase plan for the Prince Bay area at a technical meeting.

In the same year, CMG proposed the "Rebuilding a New Shekou" plan, recognized as another major development challenge for Shekou following the Reform and Opening-up.

"We hope to seize the historical opportunity of industrial transformation and upgrading in Shenzhen, and build the 11-square-kilometer Shekou into a new, business-friendly and livable coastal urban area, making it a pacesetter for regional industrial transformation and upgrading in China."
– Vision of CMG's "Rebuilding a New Shekou" plan

Dacheng Flour Factory

In 2010, with the industrial upgrading and transformation in Shekou, Dacheng Flour Factory ceased its operation.

2011

In December 2011, the land parcel K202-0014 located in the Prince Bay area of Shekou was publicly listed for sale. China Merchants Shekou Industrial Zone Holdings Co., Ltd. won the bidding, and signed the land transfer contract.

2012

In October 2012, design firms SOM and OMA were invited by CMG to participate in the consulting project for the conceptual planning and design of Prince Bay.

2013

In February 2013, SOM and OMA completed and submitted the conceptual planning and design for Prince Bay.

In May, OMA's plan was selected.

From June to December 2013, UPDIS participated in the technical review and specified the planning conditions.

In December 2013, the Detailed Blueprint phase started.

"The 'One City Three Pockets' masterplan introduces three major urban gestures – the Maritime Pocket, the Commercial Pocket, and the Community Pocket – which take geometric shapes in response to the existing coastline. Each of these pockets has distinct programing and mediates between the waterfront and the landscape city."
– Conceptual Urban Design for Prince Bay by OMA

In December 2013, the 5th Bi-City Biennale of Urbanism Architecture (UABB) in Shenzhen was held at the Float Glass Factory, a former industrial site in Shekou, triggered discussions and raised concerns about industrial heritage preservation in the area.

In 2013, CMG Shekou Industrial Zone initiated the "Shekou Relaunch" series of activities and, during the 5th UABB, held the Creative Development Strategy Forum & International Design Workshop for the Industrial Culture Zone of Dacheng Flour Factory, inviting the participation of four architects Ryue NISHIZAWA, Doreen Heng LIU, Jürgen Mayer H. and Philip F. YUAN and their firms.

"After three decades of development, Shekou has seen the early industrial buildings, which once created industrial miracle, have been deserted. In fact, those buildings are still young compared with the old factory buildings in China's industrial centers like Shanghai and Wuhan, but they are the starting points of urbanization and industrialization in Shenzhen. We always regard the history of Shekou as the greatest assets for the future development of Shekou Industrial Zone. We also cherish the industrial buildings which carry the history and culture of Shekou. Instead of consuming them, we hope to carry forward the innovative spirit of the older generation of Shekou people, make the best use of the industrial heritage to shape the future, and create our own history."
– YANG Tianping, Former General Manager of China Merchants Group Shekou Industrial Zone Co., Ltd., an interview from *d.PLUS*

2014

In April, UPDIS produced the Detailed Blueprint for Comprehensive Development of the Prince Bay Area.

In May, the Detailed Blueprint was reported to the Urban Planning, Land and Resources Commission of Shenzhen Municipality.

In November 2014, the opinions were collected, the modifications were made, and the finalized Detailed Blueprint was submitted.

2015

In August 2015, the Detailed Blueprint for Comprehensive Development of the Prince Bay Area was approved.

In March 2015, UABB announced that Dacheng Flour Factory was selected as the main exhibition venue for the 6th exhibition, and Doreen Heng LIU's team of NODE Architecture & Urbanism was responsible for its renovation design.

The construction of Dacheng Flour Factory renovation project started in June, and was completed in November.

On December 4, 2015, the 6th UABB was unveiled.

"The design principle meant to retain and strengthen the very original quality of this industrial building with distinctive features, then implant new functions. To explore and regenerate the potential and vitality of the original spaces in those seemingly generic and typical factory buildings, powerful interventions are employed to maximize their attributes and realize diverse and hierarchical spaces. While preserving and restoring the original appearance of the industrial legacy as much as possible, unique visitor circulation is also created to offer all visitors an opportunity to experience in person the traces of the once booming industry."
– Dacheng Flour Factory Innovation Design Plan by NODE Architecture & Urbanism

Since 2016, the construction of the Prince Bay area has commenced in phases.

In November 2016, the Prince Bay Cruise Homeport was opened.

"The opening of the Prince Bay Cruise Homeport marks the official entry of Shenzhen into the cruise era, which will further promote Shenzhen to become an international comprehensive transport hub and consolidate Shenzhen's important position in the Belt and Road Initiatives. The development of the cruise economy will also greatly enhance Shenzhen's momentum, influence and competitiveness."
– A speech at the Opening of China Merchants Group Cruise Homeport

2016

In February 2016, the 6th UABB closed after presenting 160 exhibits submitted by exhibitors from over 25 countries and regions around the world. According to statistics, a total of 209 cultural events were held during the exhibition period, attracting more than 250,000 visitors.

In July 2016, due to the blueprint of the area and construction of the main trunk road leading to the cruise port, Building #8, the former warehouse of China Merchants Group Port, which served as the main exhibition hall of the biennale in the Dacheng Flour Factory renovation area was demolished, causing widespread public concern.

"This Biennale has made more people realize that it is of great practical significance for Shenzhen to emphasize the use of existing urban and architectural spaces, rather than merely focusing on construction of more buildings."
–YANG Hong, Former Member of the Standing Committee of Shenzhen Municipal Committee of the CPC, a closing speech at UABB, February 28, 2016

"After getting off the car, I could hardly believe that this was the venue of the Biennale that I had just visited and marveled at a few months ago: the excavators swept across the ruins with a momentum of crushing everything; the steel drills deftly pulled down the slate-clad walls from the pile of ruins, crashing and shattering them; the banners printed with 'Re-living the City' and 'UABB' were covered with dust on walls, and others were broken and fluttered in the wind. The building that carried the memories and dreams of two generations only had the steel skeleton standing in the ruins."
– "Are We Creating a New Shenzhen by Demolishing Everything?" a report of *Shenzhener*, August 15, 2016

"The cultivation of a city's temperament and heritage requires time and patience. In the course of rapid development, if we blindly pursue speed and resolutely erase the traces of the past with no nostalgia, how could we know where we started and where we are going?"
– A message from citizen @Brody

2017

In 2017, the first year of its operation, China Merchants Group Shekou Prince Bay Cruise Homeport hit the target of 109 ship-times, carrying nearly 190,000 cruise passengers, with destinations covering 9 countries and regions.

2018

Since August 2018, CMG Shekou has conducted public listing transactions to raise capital and bring in partners for property investments. China International Marine Containers (Group) Co., Ltd. (CIMC) acquired shares in several plots in the Prince Bay area, including the plot where the Dacheng Flour Factory is located.

2019

In 2019, Building #3 and the Auditorium in the Dacheng Flour Factory renovation area were demolished one after another.

2020

In March 2020, Dacheng Flour Factory was included in the *List of Protected Historic Buildings in Shenzhen (the second batch)* announced by Shenzhen Municipal People's Government.

Apartments and office buildings in the Prince Bay area are gradually being put into use, with a highly anticipated shopping plaza – K11 Art Mall – expected to be completed in phases from 2024.

"In 2023, CIMC Industry & City Development will continue to focus on the development of the Greater Bay Area and the Yangtze River Delta, creating a number of new industrial parks and key projects, including Shenzhen CIMC Prince Bay Dacheng Plaza, to promote the development of high-quality industries in the city and bring more possibilities for quality industrial spaces."
– 2023 Product and Service Launch Conference of CIMC Industry & City Development

2021

In August 2021, Aedas won the International Competition for Industrial Heritage Renovation and Urban Renewal of the plot where Dacheng Flour Factory was located.

2022

In 2022, with the gradual development of the Prince Bay area, only the silo and the mill building were preserved in the Dacheng Flour Factory renovation area.

2023

With CIMC in charge of the development of the former Dacheng Flour Factory site, the new round of renovation has begun.

PRINCE BAY: THE HISTORICAL VIEW AND INTRINSIC LOGIC OF URBAN PLANNING

Interview with HUANG Weidong

HUANG Weidong, General Manager and Technical Director of Urban Planning & Design Institute of Shenzhen Co., Ltd., Professorate Senior Planner Engineer

Date: 1st June, 2022
Place: Urban Planning & Design Institute of Shenzhen (UPDIS)
Interviewer: Doreen Heng LIU
Editor: XIAO Caizi

The Origin of Prince Bay: a Story from 700 Years Ago

The name "Prince Bay," originated in an incident during the late years of China's Southern Song dynasty. In 1279 AD, the Southern Song army waged a fierce naval battle with the Yuan army at Ya Mountain (in the south of Xinhui District, Jiangmen, Guangdong). The Song army's forces were defeated in this decisive battle. The prime minister of Song, LU Xiufu, carrying the young emperor ZHAO Bing on his back, threw himself into the sea to commit suicide, marking the end of the Song dynasty's 319-year reign. ZHAO Bing's corpse, dressed in a yellow imperial robe, drifted to the shore near Chiwan, Shekou. An elderly monk recognized the identity of the corpse, retrieved it from the sea and gave it a ritual burial at the foot of Xiaonanshan Mountain[1]. This is what we can see today as ZHAO Bing's Mausoleum (Song Shao Di Ling) in Shenzhen, and it is from this that Prince Bay (Tai Zi Bay) got its name.

Let us stretch the yardstick of both time and space a little further again. In 1267 AD, Persian astronomer Jamal al-Din contributed a globe to the Yuan emperor. Historical material recorded that this wooden globe represented the earth as 70 percent water and 30 percent land, and bore lines of latitude and longitude.[2]

Seven hundred years ago, this was an extraordinary phenomenon, coming a whole 225 years before the globe made by Martin Behaim. Science requires imagination, and this is true imagination. Of course, historical materials may contain

1 — *Genealogy of ZHAO family · Emperor Bing* records: "Later, the remains floated to Chiwan, concealed by a flock of birds. The old monk from the ancient temple at the foot of the mountain went to the shore to inspect, and suddenly saw the unusual scene: the remains floating in the sea, with a flock of birds hovering above. He salvaged the body, and found the complexion was lifelike, and the clothing was not like those of ordinary people. He knew that it was the remains of the emperor, and he gave him a ritual burial on the sunny side of the foothills."

2 — *Yuan History · Astronomical Records, (Yuan History, Volume 48, Record One) Instrument from Western Region's* states: In the fourth year of Zhiyuan period (1267 AD), Jamal al-Din made a Instrument: Kura-i-ard, also translated as "Geographical Records" in Chinese. It was made of wood in a shape of sphere, with seventy percent representing water in color green, and thirty percent representing land in color white. The depiction included rivers, lakes, and seas, with intricate networks, and small squares were drawn to measure the surface area of the sphere and the distance of the road.

exaggerated elements, but I prefer to believe that this globe actually existed. After all, before the fall of the Southern Song dynasty, the Yuan empire already exerted significant control over the Asian continent, in the south as far as Indonesia, in the north as far as Kievan Rus, possessing extremely extensive territories. We can see global cultural interconnectedness from very early stages.

Time flies. Seven hundred years later, in 1979, Shekou unleashed the "first blast" in China's Reform and Opening-up, making it the first region to open to the world. Comrade DENG Xiaoping, the designer-in-chief of the Reform and Opening-up, amid tides of global economic transformation and significant industrial changes with acute foresight, resolutely decided to open up from Shekou, and surging development began here in this area. The Reform and Opening-up was not merely an internal reform, but China's adaptation to globalization, a critical window-opening move. Also, the Shekou Industrial Zone was not drawn by urban planners and architects; it was a giant stride by which China stretched out both arms and embraced the global community.

The Birth of Dacheng Flour Factory: The Three Supplies and One Compensation

After the birth of the Shekou Industrial Zone, the slogan "Time is Money, Efficiency is Life" became the hallmark that embodied the generation of the Shekou spirit. From the end of the 1970s to the later years of the 1980s, in the early period of construction, Shekou Industrial Zone went through a labour-intensive industrial development stage, especially with such tentative trade forms as "three supplies and one compensation," namely "processing with supplied materials, processing according to supplied samples, assembling with supplied parts, and compensation trade." What was more prominent in the Industrial Zone was the establishment of various factories by foreign capital. A number of overseas-funded factories such as Dacheng Flour Factory and Float Glass

Factory emerged accordingly, served as important pillars of Shenzhen's export-oriented economy, and becoming the epitome of the prosperous development of Shekou Industrial Zone.

The site selected for Dacheng Flour Factory was on a piece of reclaimed land on the coast of the northwest corner of Prince Bay. This site selection could be considered almost inevitable: At that time, there were rudimentary Pier-1 and Pier-2 wharves along the coast, representing the initial attempts to construct docks during the early stages of the Reform and Opening-up. Although they were far inferior to today's Shekou Port or Yantian Port, which have huge throughputs, but they sustained the functional needs of the entire area to transport cargos and construction materials during that era. The flour factory was chosen to be located next to the Pier-1 wharf in order to make the circulation of bulk grain raw materials and products optimally convenient, fast and economical.

The land reclamation was also inevitable at that time. Land bordering the coastline was extremely scarce and, as the area developed, the value of land increased. In the era of a demographic dividend from extremely abundant and inexpensive labor, large quantities of stone blasted out from Weibo Mountain were transported to the shore by manpower, reclaiming land along the coast of Prince Bay. Today it is widely acknowledged that reclamation has caused serious damage to the ecological environment of the coastline. In those days, however, under the premise of lack of awareness of marine ecological and driven by great initial development ambitions, the scale of the port in Prince Bay gradually expanded during the reclamation process.

In 1986, the master plan proposed to use "port + road" to provide transportation guarantees for the export-oriented economy of "three supplies and one compensation." As the first export-oriented industrial zone, Shekou's planning focused on the driving function of the port. From the late 1980s to the 1990s, a large number of strategic resources converged in the Prince Bay area. Large factories coalesced in the port, industry prospered, the wharves were busy and various manufacturing industries flourished. With the rapid changes in the city, however, the production and trade form of "three supplies and one compensation" gradually began to fail to adapt to high-speed socio-economic change. In the mid-1990s, the Shenzhen Municipal Government ceased approving "three supplies and one compensation" projects, and began vigorously to encourage the development of new high-tech industries, and actively guided the upgrading and transformation of existing enterprises.

Shekou Acceleration: Upgrading and Iteration

After the millenium, Shenzhen accelerated its transition of economic development from "Shenzhen speed" to "Shenzhen quality." Shekou entered a period of strategic transformation, and the integration of the bay area accelerated, giving rise to towering skyscrapers. New high-technology industries, financial services, tertiary industries and other high value-added, low resource consumption forms of new business emerged, and the number of researchers and professional technicians began to increase significantly. In comparison with the past, the structure of the urban population changed greatly, and, accordingly, supply and demand for urban services also underwent enormous changes. By about 2010, we already had reasonably good economic terrain. From the coarsely labour intensive stage, we entered the capital intensive "Made in Shenzhen" era. The manufacturing industry became extremely strong, leading also to high-end service capability beyond manufacturing industry. Over the past decade, the emphasis has shifted to "innovation." Today, innovation is already a symbolic characteristic of Shenzhen, attracting many people from all over the world to research and learn.

When the industries in Prince Bay has undergone comprehensive upgrading, and land became extremely expensive, if one wished to continue to produce flour here, to do so would clearly be ill-timed. Just as on the road traveled by industrial production in Western countries, when more advanced production emerges, industries inevitably undergo processes of internal transformation; relatively regressive or excessive production capacities will be transferred to areas where manpower and production costs are cheaper. Dacheng Flour Factory initially came to Shenzhen to reduce production and transportation costs, but now that production costs rose once again, they were continuing to set foot on the road of migration. Later, the business relocated its flour production to Henan, Tianjin, even Afghanistan. This is the fixed logic of commercial production. In 2010, Shekou's Dacheng Flour Factory, in line with industry upgrades and transformations in the area, terminated operations. The scenes of days gone by were no more, leaving behind a series of industrial buildings on the shores of Prince Bay.

The composition of industries in Shekou during this period were already very different from the earlier period. As part of the transformation, some important industrial heritage was renovated. Such as Nanhai E-Cool, a creative industrial culture park in Shekou, was once a factory of Sanyo, and the Float Glass Factory, the main venue for the 2013 Bi-City Biennale of Urbanism\Architecture (UABB). These changes reflected the city's significant economic evolution. People in Shekou became increasingly aware of the value of this land, with its prominent geographical and ecological strengths, nestled between mountains and seas. Our city, moreover, had already entered a period of relatively high-end development, and would need all the better to engage in dialogue with the entire world.

In 2015, the Qianhai-Shekou Free Trade Zone was established, marking a new era for Shekou as it shifted its focus towards technological innovation, cultural creativity and financial services, presenting a new international face. Prince Bay faced a huge opportunity of Shenzhen-Hong Kong cooperation, becoming a new center in the integration and development of the bay area, transforming into a comprehensive urban area. In the same year, Dacheng Flour Factory was selected as the main venue for the 6th edition of UABB. Amid the unique background of Shekou as "the Special Zone within the Special Zone," Dacheng Flour Factory, which carried Shenzhen's original development memory, welcomed the highlight moment of renovation and rebirth.

Revitalizing an Industrial Heritage vs. The Dream of a Cruise Home Port

Looking back to the 1980s, to be able to manufacture high-grade flour in Shenzhen was considered to be absolutely tremendous. To be able also to sell it overseas amounted already to the fulfilment of a dream for that era. Shenzhen, as it entered the twenty-first century, ranked number one Chinese global trading city for more than ten consecutive years, had already truly connected to the world. When various trades and technological innovations occur here, when the area generates higher economic and globalized distribution needs, the magnificent dream of a cruise liner home port was born.

At the beginning of the twenty-first century, Urban Planning & Design Institute of Shenzhen (UPDIS) was commissioned by China Merchants Group to start a new round of planning for Prince Bay. At the time, many matters were uncertain, but there was a leaning towards a promising new blueprint. Many rounds of different plans were developed during that period, and many changes were made during each round. The cruise home port construction and operation was a highly specialized global supply chain project, requiring, for judgment, the bringing of an even broader perspective, not merely the building of a new terminal. Questions arose: Where do the cruise liners come from? Where do the customers come from? What are the customers' expectations?

What would the customers do after they arrived? This was a set of issues of strict commercial logic. At the time, we suggested seeking partners worldwide with similar work experience to prepare a business plan, and what happened next was the launch of a spatial design competition.

In 2014, therefore, there was an international consulting project for Prince Bay planning, in which OMA and SOM participated, with OMA eventually winning the bid. The subsequent detailed planning was carried out by UPDIS. At the time, OMA's plan was outstanding but also highly controversial. I believe this plan showcased a kind of "desire" as China reached its summit in economic transformation. This word "desire" may not be pleasing to hear, but as the saying goes, "the mind reveals itself through the appearance." When the internal capital power has reached a certain extent, the spatial form that takes shape is indeed like that.

It's worth pointing out that, in 2013-2014, China Merchants Group, organized an International Design Workshop on Creative Development for Dacheng Industrial Heritage Project, inviting four architects Ryue NISHIZAWA, Doreen Heng LIU, Jürgen Mayer H. and Philip F. YUAN to participate. They explored the line of thought of transforming Dacheng Flour Factory as a creative and cultural base, and presented conceptual renovation proposals.
This workshop also became an opportunity for Doreen Heng LIU with her studio NODE Architecture & Urbanism to undertake Dacheng Flour Factory renovation for UABB in 2015. The workshop was carried out concurrently with OMA's plan at the time. China Merchants Group allowed these events to proceed at the same time, signifying that they were both very important. It was a very comprehensive form of consideration. As regards the final decision, it was all the more the entire city development's internal power mechanism exerting its effect.

As a state-owned enterprise, China Merchants Group has always assumed a role similar to urban governance in Shekou, effectively managing the area in various aspects such as urban space, functional iterations, healthcare and public services. China Merchants Group is a very typical sample in China's modernization process. Since its establishment 150 years ago, it has been embracing the world and confronting modernization head-on. There have always been two threads to China Merchants Group: On one hand, it is commercially oriented; it strives to pursuing profits and maximize land value. On the other hand, China Merchants Group also has a strong cultural inclination. These forces occur simultaneously and balance each other. At Prince Bay, therefore, we can see a powerful planning image feature which comes from OMA, with a global and even universal orientation, and we can also witness researches and discussions with a cultural emphasis on the industrial heritage of Dacheng Flour Factory.

Let us return to the OMA case. In the beginning, OMA was not concerned with the fate of Dacheng Flour Factory, however, as urban planners, we never gave up the thread of retaining the plant. Later, I recommended Rocco S.K. YIM to further develop the initial plan, because his deliberations in relation to culture would be more comprehensive. Our efforts was not for the sake of showcasing or hosting a biennale exhibition, but rather a genuine hope to preserve the memory of the city. The Factory had once represented a significant milestone in China's modernization process.

"Inevitable Demolitions"

As one of the most important "power source" areas of the special zone, the evolution and rise of Shekou are directly related to the economic dynamics of the city behind it. The conventional business operation is to seek to maximize profits, tear down the old things and reconstructing, showing a flourishing new look; but cultural and academic circles believe that the world should be more diverse, and that a city is more organic and vibrant when elements from various historical periods are intertwined. The starting points of the two ways of thinking are completely different.

As to the subsequent demolition of the Building #8 and a series of other buildings in the Dacheng Flour Factory area, I won't define these as good or bad; more particularly it was more of an inevitability. When this area attracted more advanced industries, the value that the future promised to generate reached a much higher level than before. Amid such strong economic forces, Building #8 and other additional buildings were demolished one after the other. What is very interesting is that the Silos and the Mill Building were preserved not because the cultural and academic circles said, "Don't demolish them." The decision to retain them was primarily influenced by two factors. Firstly, the large dimension of the Silos made the cost of demolition prohibitively high. Secondly, they are located next to the pier, which was not ideal for the area's intended use, led to their preservation for the time being. This decision was largely driven by market economics.

Building #8 seemed like a relatively old structure with a simple frame, which, at the first glance, left little to the imagination. At the same time, the brand new, wide road was very important; it led directly to the cruise liner home port, and, in the future, a large number of vehicles and public transportation systems would shuttle back and forth here. NODE once proposed a plan to let the road pass through Building #8, but this method of simultaneously preserving the road and the building was ultimately not adopted. I absolutely believe that the road could pass through the building, but this needed time to discuss and investigate. When deciding the fate of Building #8, there was not so much time, and there was not so much top-down forces saying, "This matter is very important. You should study the feasibility." All these reasons led to the result that was demolition. When accelerating towards the great dream of the cruise liner home port, the slogan "Time is Money, Efficiency is Life" suddenly came to mind again – time, time, time... In fact, this is a very preliminary ideology, relied on a crude sense of urgency.

Later we saw that in urban regeneration in Shanghai, some similar "win-win" schemes had been realized. Shanghai's capacity for urban governance is far greater than that of a city that is only 40 years old, giving all stakeholders enough time to ponder. Our city is still very young, and its cultural context is relatively rough, which lead to a series of problems. The roughness, combined with the internalized cultural temperament, governance capacity and tolerance of the city, forms a restrictive structure, in which it is not simply to want to do well or not to do well, to preserve or not to preserve. Our cities need to be a little bit more patient. Don't rush to fill in every gap. Leave some time for it to ferment properly, grow some new elements, and let it age.

An Interwined Path of the Old and the New

When a great, civilized, ancient country seeks to modernize in the faces of global modernization, it becomes extremely challenging. Why? Because China's traditional cultural foundation runs deep. During the May 4th New Culture Movement in 1919, there was a fervent wave of demolishing everything old, people enthusiastically "smash the old and bring in the new." On one hand, they denied traditions, but, on the other hand, they had not yet had the time to create and innovate. They could only imitate and appropriate foreign concepts and language. This undoubtedly made the process of innovation very difficult and left behind many repercussions. In his later years, HU Shi, an emblematic figure of the May 4th Movement, actually returned to study traditional culture. Our cultural heritage is so rich and profound that we cannot simply and directly distinguish or criticize the good and the bad, the new and the old. With thousands of years of heritage, it is very difficult for us to embrace modernization.

Under the impact of modernization, a mainstream concept holds that new is good, that it's advanced, while old is bad or even obsolete. This complex has continued to this day, and people delight in witnessing the rapid changes in the city. In the 1970s and 1980s, crude video halls and karaoke lounges were the typical scenes of new urban life at that time. Today in a city like Shenzhen, people aspire to have a large cruise port that features geometrically shaped buildings, serving as a gateway connecting the world. To some extent, this is a shared consciousness that influences our choices.

Most people don't understand the "three supplies and one compensation" now. Most of the early buildings that emerged during the Reform and Opening-up have been demolished and replaced with brand new shopping malls and mansions. In just 40 years, the first batch of industrial plant represented by Dacheng Flour Factory have become outdated structures in this rapidly evolving city. What is very interesting is that Dacheng Flour Factory produced flour for baking. These products, as important food raw materials, actually nurtured Shenzhen, which was a frontier city in mainland China at that time, as well as China's Hong Kong and Macau, both as part of the Pearl River Delta. Of course, this may be far-fetched, but I always feel that the factory has a special and profound connection with the city – the original industrial imprint of the city, together with other extensive industries, nurtured and nourished the city, much like a "mother." The "mother" of the city should not be erased, and traces of the past should be retained. These remnants and new things can together form a relatively complex and vibrant district, presenting the true essence of Shekou's earliest exploration as a pioneer in the Reform and Opening-up era.

Today's neighborhoods in Shekou have streets on a pleasant scale and beautiful public spaces, and they are not intentionally designed this way. In the early days of industrialization, this area was a barren land. At that time, China was still an agricultural country, and we didn't have much concept of the construction of transportation infrastructure such as overpasses, expressways, and large freight facilities. A road width of about 10 meters was sufficient. Fortunately, these streets have been kept, so the small-scale street life naturally grows from here, which was actually unintentional.

As regards some of the "old" in the city's current situation, we will know their origins after looking back properly. This is actually the most important matter in relation to our design and planning work. If we don't see these sources, we may mistakenly believe that humans can conquer nature, or we can use better and more comprehensive planning and design concepts to transform everything. I hope we don't always think about tearing down all the old buildings, but can accommodate the old beauty and conform to the favorable relationship between people and the city.

Boundaries and Intrinsic Dynamics of Public Policy and Planning

In the past, the planning community particularly emphasized the relationship between spatial axes, spatial agglomeration, commanding heights, landmarks and skylines; however in the new era, when undertaking urban design in Shenzhen, we focus on the concept of "one cross-city ridge, one coastal belt, eight hills and ten waterways,"[3] which gives greater prominence to the ecological environment and public spaces, and how these spaces can be more conveniently utilized to better serve the needs of people. It reflects a shift in the values of urban planning and design

3 — In 2017, the *Shenzhen Comprehensive Urban Design and Feature Protection Strategy Research Project* proposed to construct "a homeland facing the world," build an ecological space framework and form a "continuous, complete and systematic" ecological protection layout. The charming ecological framework including one green ridge, one coastal blue belt, eight mountain corridors, 10 water corridors, together with over 100 city paths and more than 1,000 parks, jointly create a harmonious, beautiful and livable home in Shenzhen.

towards respecting nature and prioritizing people's well-being. With such values, our cities will move along the road to true sustainable development.

In 2020, in the work related to the overall urban design of Shenzhen, we proposed the idea of amplifying the urban history and imprints that emerged during the Reform and Opening-up, enhancing the humanistic depth of Shenzhen as a pioneering city, form a multi-layered history and a diverse culture, and a more distinctive urban landscape. We delineated 29 distinctive conservation zones under five categories: mountain and sea settlements, Lingnan towns, reform windows, urban villages, creative industrial parks. The planning strategy aims to comprehensively restore the functions of historical buildings, integrate modern lifestyles, and provide creative spaces with moderate costs to attract innovative enterprises and talents. This is an important orientation for urban design in Shenzhen today, and it is a basic value. Under such a premise, industrial heritages such as Dacheng Flour Factory can truly be incorporated into the public policy. Sometimes we have to understand that public policy may be more important than design alone, because once the protection of public policy takes effect, it is a systematic, reasonable and legal protection.

I have consistently emphasized that urban planning is a social and public affair, and there must be boundaries in terms of space management and control. It is not appropriate to expand the boundaries infinitely, and the market must be left with sufficient flexibility to allocate various elements and resources. Meanwhile, public policy should become the "gatekeeper" of the public domain, by, for example, exercising strict and effective management and control of streets, public spaces, historical and cultural blocks, etc., without intervening excessively in the "private" space. This "private" falls within quotation marks because our land is state-owned; this is in fact something of a vague concept. The governance of Chinese cities is different from that in Western countries. It is a common value formed by various complex factors such as a unique society, economy, politics, and culture.

When looking at the progress of civilization, planners need to see a larger scope. These processes are not drawn on paper, but are evolved and promoted by the power intrinsic to the development of society and economy, the evolution of cities and the iteration of industries. A good planner needs to seek a larger space for maneuver and relatively scientific solutions amidst constraints. Perhaps by persisting until the end, they can truly achieve valuable outcomes, however, such success is not the planner convincing the decision-makers, but complying with the logic of urban governance and maintaining scientific common sense and logic. Sometimes planners and designers form good solutions, and eventually some of them may be adopted, which can be considered progress.

The top-level design of Shenzhen's public policy also benefited from the discussion and efforts of the architectural and planning professions, academia, and cultural sector, so it is important for people to speak out. The Biennale held that year at the Dacheng Flour Factory also established such values, which was a demonstration of the significance of the times; it was not a declaration in a purely academic sense, but a concrete action to preserve urban culture.

Towards a Complex Urban Culture

The future of this region is promising. Our city is moving towards complexity, and with the progress of society, people will be more and more eager for cultural nourishment. They will return to the origins of the city, to explore the industrial heritages of the early days of the Reform and Opening-up, and to re-understand the significance of places like Dacheng Flour Factory, to experience the special character brought about by the interweaving of different cultures in this place. This is a complex experience with a sense of conflict and the sediment of time. If no one wants to enjoy the Biennale, there may never be a highlight moment in which Dacheng Flour Factory appears at the Biennale to captivate people's eyes and hearts.

I believe a good city must be rich in historical vestiges, with ample continuity and timeliness. From the perspective of urban history and culture or the persistence of cultural context in architecture, we must strive to retain these spatial carriers and environments that have played a role in a certain period; at least to make deliberate choices to retain them to the greatest extent possible, so that we can witness a city rich in culture, instead of a place that is always brand new. Such a place lacks the threads of time and is bound to be dull. These old buildings and places can remind us immediately of the story of this city and this piece of land.

What is urban culture? Isn't it when we reflect on the history of the city, we can see a multitude of stories layered within its spatial memory, reminding us how rich and interesting our city is? The story says, centuries ago, the young Emperor of Song Dynasty perished in Yashan, drifted to this very place wearing a yellow robe, and his body was buried at the foot of the mountain. That was an event 700 years before the first blast of the Reform and Opening-up in Shekou. Later, piers and factories were built here, carrying the glory of the Special Economic Zone and forging ahead towards modernization with unwavering determination. Today, these buildings are still here. With rejuvenated vitality and profound significance, they are integrating into the new era.

THE PLANNING SCHEME FOR PRINCE BAY: CONCEIVING A BLUEPRINT FOR PRINCE BAY AS AN INTERNATIONAL CALLING CARD

2000 – 2015

Urban Planning & Design
Institute of Shenzhen

- **Connecting the coastal vitality belt:** The waterfront area integrates residential, commercial, and port functions, with creative offices and corporate headquarters. The three representative spacial symbols are: circle (sea-front residence), rectangle (K11 Art Mall), and triangle (the cruise home port).

- **Connecting the coastline:** A 15-kilometer coastal leisure belt extends from Sea World to Prince Bay, creatively integrating elements such as natural landscapes (mangroves and coastal scenery), ports, production, and technological innovation.

- **Traffic improvements:** The metro line terminating near Prince Bay is planned to further integrate with the Qianhai Area. Simultaneously, the original ferry terminal will be relocated and expanded. An international cruise home port is also planned to enhance international connectivity.

- **Integrating industrial heritages and maritime tourism:** This area blends new construction with renovation efforts while preserving the silos of Dacheng Flour Factory, positioning as one of Shenzhen's hallmarks.

2000:

Renovation Concept Plan for Prince Bay Area (Pier 1)

Integrating its traditional cultural origin, the area was named Prince Bay, and the planning includes residential zones, coastal tourism and commercial service areas, and high-tech financial office district.

2002:

Revised Renovation Concept Plan for Prince Bay Area

Establishing a comprehensive transfer center in Shenzhen, integrating four types of passenger terminals (Hong Kong and Macau, domestic high-speed passenger ships, ferries and cruise ships), metros, public transport and related property services. The plan aims to develop a Shekou CBD integrated with Sea World, leveraging logistics and people flow. It focuses on shaping public open spaces and waterfront activity areas to cater to the needs of citizens, creating a comprehensive, modern, subtropical seaside coastal community for leisure, sightseeing, business, and residence.

2007:

Detailed Blueprint for Prince Bay Area

Building a Shekou CBD integrated with Sea World, shaping the public open space and waterfront activity area, catering to the needs of citizens, and creating a comprehensive, modern, subtropical, seaside coastal community for leisure, sightseeing, business and residence. At the same time, it aims to establish a future fashion and lifestyle experience district for Shenzhen citizens.

2009:

Revised Detailed Blueprint for Prince Bay Area Comprehensive Development Project

The area was positioned as a comprehensive development area integrating international business and commerce, culture and leisure, and serving as a low-carbon demonstration area with coordinated development of economy, society, and environment, creating the four functional systems of a high-end business platform, a coastal leisure coastline, an international cruise home port and a transportation transit hub.

2014:

Conceptual Plan and Design for Prince Bay Comprehensive Development Project

Through "one city" and "three pockets," the elements of commerce, office, hotel, business apartment, residence, cruise terminal, international hospital and school spaces are combined to create a year-round dynamic area that is livable, comfortable and suited to tourism. It is the first truly international-level development zone in Shenzhen and even in China.

2015:
Revised Detailed Blueprint for Prince Bay Area Comprehensive Development Project

The area was positioned as "Qianhai Pioneering Area, LOHAS Harbour City" and aims to become an important maritime gateway to Shenzhen, a model area of Shenzhen-Hong Kong cooperation, and a LOHAS city suitable for residence and business.

Masterplan of Prince Bay

OMA, 2014

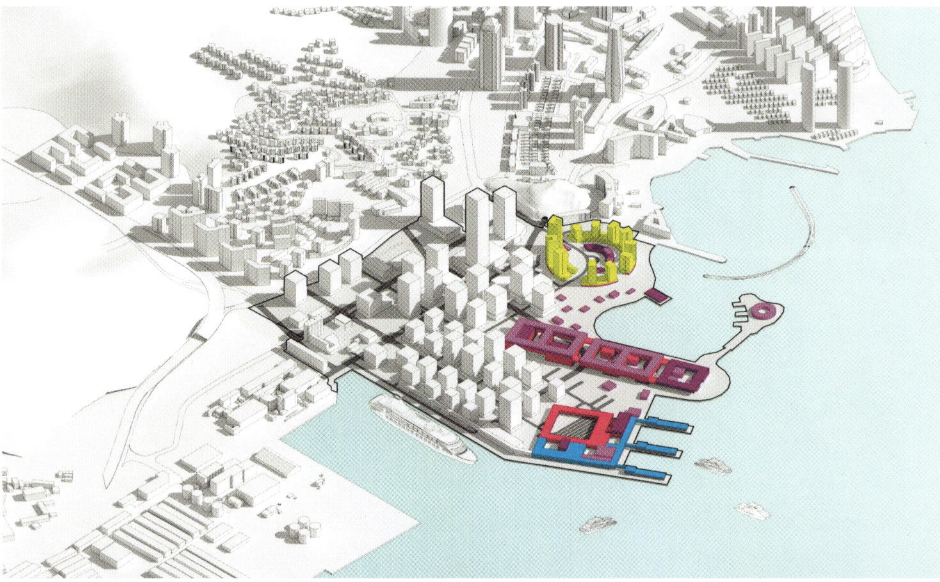

01

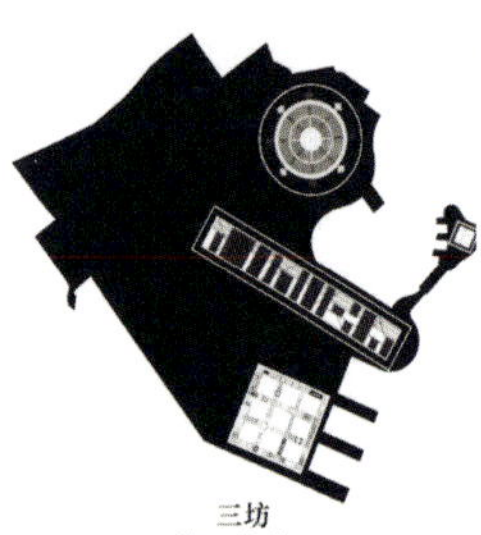

02

03

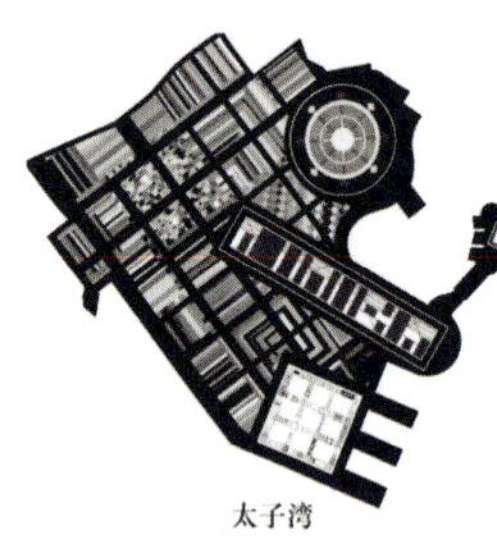

01 The masterplan introduces three major urban gestures–the Maritime Pocket, the Commercial Pocket, and the Community Pocket–which take geometric shapes in response to the existing coastline. Each of these pockets has distinct programming and mediates between the waterfront and the landscape city.

02 The landscape city provides a setting for the three pockets. Within the uniform grid established by the road network, zones of public green space occur within city blocks and at major intersections. The regular layout provides accessibility and flexible uses, while enhancing navigation within the site.

03 The synergy between the landscape city and the pockets creates diverse, functional and human-oriented environments, rejuvenating Prince Bay as a significant point of access into China.

II. WORKSHOP

Relaunching the industrial heritage

Since the turn of the millennium, the city has witnessed constant and dynamic transformations. The factories that had been established during the early days of the Reform and Opening-up gradually ceased their operations, bringing about the conflicts between the old and new urban fabrics. Should these buildings be demolished or preserved? That was the question.

In 2013, the Float Glass Factory in Shekou Industrial Zone was selected as the main venue for the 5th Bi-City Biennale of Urbanism\Architecture, garnered attention to and sparked discussions on the old industrial buildings in the zone. To preserve the historical and industrial cultural value of Dacheng Flour Factory in the same area, China Merchants Shekou Industrial Zone organized design workshops and lectures. In this endeavor, four architects, Ryue NISHIZAWA, Doreen Heng LIU, Jürgen Mayer H., and Philip F. YUAN, were invited to contribute their insights. They proposed diverse planning and design concepts, exploring different possibilities to shape the future of Dacheng Flour Factory.

BEFORE RENOVATION

In 2011, Dacheng Flour Factory ceased operations, leaving behind the empty buildings of its once-thriving facilities. With the 2013 UABB held in the nearby Float Glass Factory gaining widespread attention for industrial heritages, Shekou Industrial Zone also incorporated the transformation of Dacheng Flour Factory into its plans. The pre-renovation status as an industrial relic sparked boundless imagination about its potential revitalization.

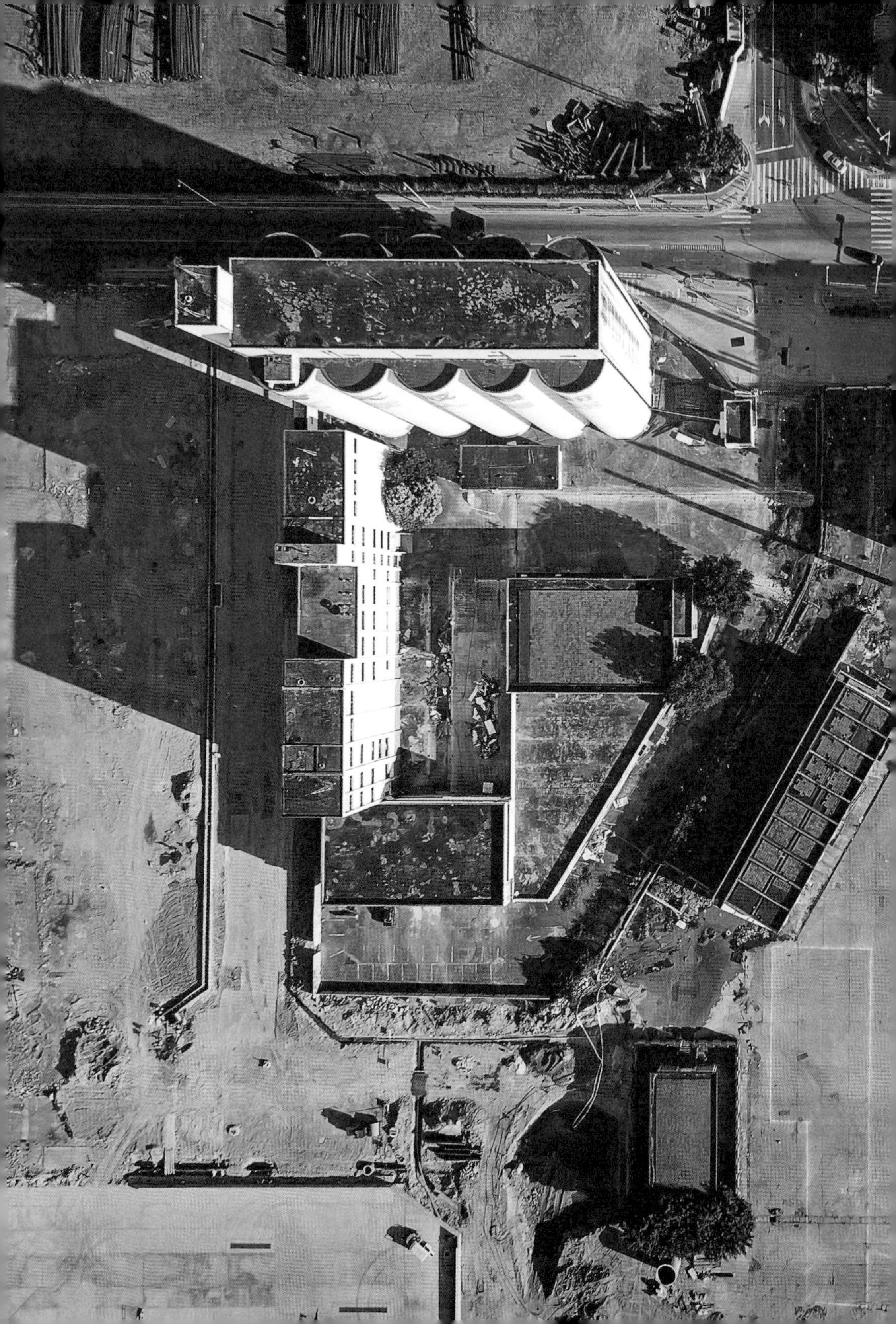

拆
拆

KATO

禁止烟火

Silos: The Former Barn

大成麵粉

麪粉
麪粉

SHEKOU RELAUNCH: CITY, PEOPLE, LIFE

Interview with ZHENG Yulong

ZHENG Yulong served as the Genaral Manager of Department of Planning and Land Development of China Merchants Shekou Industrial Zone Co.,LTD from 2013 to 2015.

Excerpted from *d.PLUS* Vol.026, May 2014
Interviewer/Editor: Domus Design Center

As described by urbanist Lewis Mumford, "the city is a theater of social action", and "or it may, through the deliberate efforts of art, politics, and education, make the drama more richly significant, as a stage-set, well-designed, intensifies and underlines the gestures for nothing that men have dwelt so often on the beauty or the ugliness of cities: these attributes qualify men's social activities." This view enlightens urban operators to pay attention to the significance of cultural activities. Such cultural activities not only enrich urban social action, but also shape up temperament and soul of a city. This interview on "Shekou Relaunch" Campaign, is to introduce the achievements made by Shekou in leveraging culture to push forward urban development.

d.PLUS: "Shekou Relaunch" series and the 2013 Bi-City Biennale of Urbanism\Architecture (UABB) are important cultural events for Shekou recently. As an enterprise, what is the starting point for China Merchants Group to plan or organize such cultural activities in Shekou Industrial Zone?

ZHENG Yulong: At the beginning of the Reform and Opening-up, China Merchants Group successfully developed the 10.85 km^2 Shekou Industrial Zone. As the first development zone opening to the outside, Shekou Industrial Zone has once led China's reforming process, and done beneficial explorations for urbanization. After 30 years of development and construction, Shekou has developed from a small fishing village to an outbound port industrial zone, and then become a beautiful coastal city area now.

In the face of new challenges and new opportunities of industrial upgrading and urban regeneration, Shekou Industrial Zone put forward the "Rebuilding a New Shekou" project in 2010. We hope to solve the new problems that Shekou faced in the redevelopment, and to explore a new road of urbanization that can represent the direction of China's industrial upgrading and urban regeneration. The "Relaunch" today places greater emphasis on development with cultural connotation, focusing more on people-oriented needs, as cultural development is key to enhancing the core competitiveness of cities.

This edition of UABB, as an international biennale, is planned to organize as a unique cultural event by integrating with Shekou's humanistic history and distinctive spatial venue, so as to catalyze chain reaction in urban development. Thus, Shekou Industrial Zone not only provides venues and supportive services, but also invests in urban transformation and actively participate in the biennale activities. "Shekou Relaunch" not only comes from the biennale exhibition, but also catalyzes it. From March 2013, these activities have held seven sessions so far. This year's activities last for nearly one year, which span the period of the biennale exhibition. Activities include architectural planning workshops and vanguard artistic activities, in line with the vanguard explorative spirit of the biennale exhibition, as well as combining Shekou's humanistic history and urban development.

At the same time, as an open platform, it invited a large number of experts, scholars, cultural creators, artists, and the public to participate and interact with various parties. The event resembled a symphony for Shekou's relaunch, starting from proposing a topic for reflection, focusing on the issue, exploring and practicing, and then returning to problem-solving.

d.PLUS: Some of the events, such as contemporary dance performance "Night of Red," Hip-Hop competition "Hustle and Freeze," and educational workshop "Creative Light Shekou", are held in the abandoned Dacheng Flour Factory, while the venues for UABB exhibition are located in the former Float Glass Factory and the original Shekou Port. Why do you select these deserted industrial plants to hold the activities?

ZHENG Yulong: Shekou Industrial Zone has only 35 years of history. However, it plays an extraordinary role in China's economic reform history. Float Glass Factory, Dacheng Flour Factory and other industrial buildings in Shekou also has only about 30 years of history. These buildings are the original points of Shenzhen's urbanization and industrialization. How could we preserve the centenary history if we don't protect this 30-year history now? These worn-out and deserted factories represent Shenzhen's urbanization development history and humanistic history of China's economic Reform and Opening-up. They imply amazing spatial power and unforgettable venue spirit.

We select these sites aiming to arouse people to re-know these venues and carry out Shekou's history and spirits. On the other hand, through the introduction and activation of new culture and innovative activities, we intend to revitalize these areas and explore realistic and historic values, so as to drive industrial transformation and promote urban vitality. Through the biennale exhibition, we aim to make these factories reproduce culture and innovation. Through the continuous events, these factory areas will become more attractive. Events such as contemporary dance performances and Hip-Hop competitions infuse the plant with a new vibe and vitality, while educational workshops transform the industrial site into a venue for family-friendly community activities.

d.PLUS: The transformation and reuse of industrial buildings often sparks controversy internationally: should they be demolished or preserved? How should they be protected? How much should be transformed? And how should they be utilized after transformation? Shekou Industrial Zone has undoubtedly encountered many debates and has taken into account the opinions of numerous experts on this issue. Can you please elaborate on how Shekou make today's decisions?

ZHENG Yulong: Indeed, the protection, utilization and transformation of industrial plants have many technical and economic problems. Our decisions should be based on specific situations. In the second phase of "Shekou Relaunch" workshop, Prof. Joan BUSQUETS claimed that "it's significant and valuable to preserve Shekou's collective memory and history, rather than creating a new urban environment."

In inheriting the history, we don't just simply preserve the architectural form. More importantly, we work with architects to explore the spirit transmitted by the venues. Tadao ANDO once said, "Creative design could re-present a period of lost history." This is a kind of "venue spirit" in people's collective memory. In addition, we carefully explore new suitable functions while protecting old buildings. Through functional utilization, we try to revitalize the buildings and achieve practical protection and development.

Now, we invite four architects to explore this, including Ryue NISHIZAWA, Doreen Heng LIU, Jürgen Mayer H. and Philip F. YUAN. We aim to develop the former site of Dacheng Flour Factory into a new humanistic landmark of Shekou and a vanguard art and cultural center.

d.PLUS: Architects responsible for the renovation of the Float Glass Factory as the 2013 UABB Venue mentioned that from the initial design stage, they had already considered leaving room for the venues to be repurposed after the Biennale. What's the plan for these venues in the post-exhibition period?

ZHENG Yulong: The 2013 UABB achieved unprecedented success, with the number of visitors exceeding 180,000. It has garnered acclaim from experts and media both domestically and internationally, being regarded as a biennial exhibition that meets top-tier international standards. It can be said that through the Biennale and the "Shekou Relaunch" activities, more people have come to see the value, hope, and future of these old factory areas, and to some extent, these events have begun to activate the development of these districts.

However, urban regeneration and industrial upgrading are also comprehensive projects that require systematic planning and implementation. Now we are executing a series of short-term, middle-term and long-term development plans. For example, we will implement an industrial design port and a trendsetter wharf to extend the vitality of the biennale exhibition. These two projects are short-term based and could generate benefits in a short time. They will promote to gather and develop industrial design and cultural creative industries by using current venue space.

In combining with middle and short term projects, we will accelerate the development of Dacheng Flour Factory after one year of planning through the exhibition. This project will become a cultural landscape in the Prince Bay area. It will extend the spirit of "Shekou Relaunch" activities and develop into a vanguard art design center and a life style experiencing center with international cultural atmosphere.

In the middle and long term aspect, on the one hand, we have started to plan the exhibition surrounding areas to solve transport, supporting facility and function problems. Academic institutions such as Harvard University and Chinese University of Hong Kong and local planning agencies have started their related works. On the other hand, we explore the possibility of inviting design institutes, innovative centers, art museums and other influential cultural and educational projects to settle down here.

d.PLUS: In interviews with the organizers of the "Shekou Relaunch" activities, it was widely acknowledged that Shekou has been very bold and inclusive in selecting the events. However, concerns were raised about whether this creative and ambitious direction can be sustained in the long term. In the near future, will Shekou continue its exploration in establishing urban cultural brands? What cultural activities are planned or will be held?

ZHENG Yulong: Shekou has gained a reputation for its pioneering spirit ever since the early days of the Reform and Opening-up. In "Shekou Relaunch" events we have made deliberate efforts to select cultural events that are avant-garde, forward-thinking, and innovative. This is not only a way to carry forward the Shekou spirit but also an integral part of Shekou's culture itself.

Through one year of hosting activities, we have built the cultural brand. To raise a city's cultural brand is to improve the city's core competitiveness. We need to expand brand influence and catalyze urban vitality in order to successfully transfer Shekou Industrial Zone's development model and to develop Shekou into a model coastal city area in China. Based on our previous experience, Shekou Industrial Zone will continuously strengthen the development of urban cultural brand. We will hold a series of events, such as urban architectural activities, vanguard cultural activities, coastal city living activities and international creative cultural community activities, such as China-France innovation forum, European gourmet festival and various performance shows. We will expand cultural influence and accelerate Shekou's transformation.

INTERNATIONAL DESIGN WORKSHOP ON CREATIVE DEVELOPMENT FOR DACHENG INDUSTRIAL HERITAGE PROJECT

2014

Excerpted from *d.PLUS* Vol.026 May 2014
Editor: Domus Design Center

Text and images of the proposals are provided by the respective architectural teams.

At present, Urban regeneration is an inevitable issue for most cities in China: Resource-based cities need to change economic growth mode, while current industrial cities need to put a new face on sectors. However, major demolition and reconstruction, destruction of history and blind scale-up of cities without restraint are widely criticized. The case of Dacheng Flour Factory make clear Shekou's approach to handling relationship between the past and the future in the wave of urban regeneration. In the Task Plan for Transformation of Shekou Dacheng Flour Factory, "fully embodying architectural features of Shekou Dacheng Flour Factory," "echoing with surrounding urban space," "public open park," "clarification for exploitation and use of land" and "synergy with the overall development mode" are put forward as five design principles. This fully sets the direction of urban regeneration in Shekou: attaching importance to urban characteristics, respecting the livable scale and insisting on "City Oriented to People."

In order to keep the historical and industrial value of Dacheng Flour Factory, Shekou Industrial Zone has organized a "Design Workshop of International Invitations for Shekou Dacheng Industrial Culture Project" and "Architect Lectures", and issued invitations to a number of well-known international firms on behalf of the Workshop to collect designs. Architects joining in the Workshop include Ryue NISHIZAWA (From Japan, 2010 Pritzker Prize winner, SANAA firm partner), Doreen Heng LIU (From Shenzhen, China, Chief Architect of NODE Architecture & Urbanism, part-time Associate Professor of School of Architecture of Chinese University of Hong Kong), Jürgen Mayer (From Germany, founder and Chief Architect of J.MAYER H. Architectural Design Studio), Philip F. YUAN (From Shanghai, China, Chief Architect of ARCHI-UNION ARCHITECTS, Associate Professor, CAUP, Tongji University).

The architect teams adopt a negotiation-interaction mode, and the Workshop also invites international specialists in architectural conservation, cultural and creative industries operations, architectural culture and art development, urban planning and other aspects to make open discussions in order to produce constructive advices on project positioning, development strategy and unique features. Professor CHEN Fuyan of Department of Mass Communication of Taiwan Tamkang University emphasizes that the key point in this case is the humanity and sociality. That is how to make the history and humanity of this place taken seriously. Director of Shenzhen Public Art Center, HUANG Weiwen, who has been involved in urban planning and management in Shenzhen for years believes doing transformation test and trial on the existing industrial plants along the Gangwan Avenue should be more viable and surer. Rome MAXXI Architecture Museum senior curator Pippo CIORRA remarks that all these four designs reflect their responses to small-scaled and low-density environment of Shekou. General Manager of Land Planning and Development Department ZHENG Yulong thinks the series of activities held reflects the ideas of

Ryue Nishizawa
刘 珩

unbearable lightness of time
bearable heaviness of space

research on this place. This place has a strong adaptability as well as many values that can be tapped, so the designs, programs and actions should reflect the culture of this place. General Manager of Shekou Industrial Zone YANG Tianping concluded that Shekou does not want to become a CBD, neither to copy any of the so-called unique places in Shenzhen.

The Workshop proposed the direction for the four architects' teams to explore, including the arts, conservation, sustainable development, creation and use of spatial characteristics, approaches, cultural heritage, spiritual values and methods of use. On this basis, the four design teams carried out the second round design. With the issue of further designs on February 26, 2014, the four chief architects presented their programs respectively. The culture embodiment raised by the Workshop has been cleverly reflected in four different forms.

PROPOSAL OF NODE ARCHITECTURE & URBANISM

Dacheng Flour Factory is located at the junction of the 1980s old industrial factory area and the future new planning area near the Cruise Homeport. With a blend of old and new urban fabrics, it reflecting a diversity of buildings within the block. The interpretation of history, whether as a future deletion and coverage of the past or as a past encumbrance and useless addition to the future, remains subjective.

Our design strategy attempts to blend and embed the future into the past, to incubate mutual growth and foster complementarity between them. The new planning and buildings explore multifaceted, flexible possibilities while respecting historical fabrics and logic.
At the urban design level, the conterminous ground of the area and its interface with the city adopt a simple checkerboard landscape that is flexible and open. This design integrates old and new buildings with diverse characteristics and aesthetics from different periods, transforming the factory district into a place that cannot be easily defined but is intriguing and lively to visitors.

At the urban reconstruction level, our strategy employs a "light touch" technique for convenient area renovation while preserving its original spatial features as much as possible. Key transformations focus on revitalizing the silos and the mill building, while the new buildings consist of distinctive units of various shapes and sizes. These new structures also can be individually completed by different architects according to functional needs, adhering to the design principles.

EXHIBITION

The silos, as the landmark in this area, its heavy concrete texture expresses the history and power. In order to save the industrial inwardness of Dacheng, the appearance of the silo is to be maintained. Thus, we plan to reorganize the inner space and make a light addition to the top; The mill building is a spatialization of the whole process technology of flour processing, and its form is a direct reaction to the process technology and reflects the logic that the form of industrial buildings act up to functions. While renovating the mill building, we also follow this principle to replace new functions to the relevant processing spaces and construct a new flow line. The rich space inside the mill building is expressed while the industrial memory is kept.

In short, the original featured units are the unique history and space resources of Dacheng Flour Factory and the future space will be merely superposed and collaged. How to carry the space collage and how to reproduce are the two sides of the same coin? The re-balance of the featured multiple units and the balance of the new productive consumption chain are the key points of Dacheng's rebirth and also the starting and finishing points of this design plan.

PROPOSAL OF ARCHI-UNION ARCHITECTS

The reconstruction of Dacheng Flour Factory plays a crucial role as a key connecting point between the glorious history of the Shekou Industrial Zone and the brand-new future of the Prince Bay area. It serves as infrastructure for urban public activities, balancing certainty and ambiguity — retaining its vitality amidst the continuous changes in surrounding functions while providing a free, high-quality meeting place.

We aim to create an "urban living room" that looks toward the future of city life. While the border of Dacheng Flour Factory is redefined by the newly planned, evenly distributed streets and blocks, we transform the factory from a single industrial function into a vibrant part of the new urban culture. Our goal is to establish an urban spatial form that accommodates diverse functions, distinct from traditional public spaces. It serves not only as a support for daily public life, like streets or gardens, but also for large-scale urban activities, such as squares and parks. The space is remodeled with flexibility, creating a complex and impressive joint of urban spaces.

The introverted, enclosed space is shaped by the preserved buildings and new street outlines, while the newly constructed public areas are redefined to meet flexible and diverse functional requirements. With a dynamic vertical park centered around naturally enclosed spaces, the entire street block becomes a multi-functional, high-density, high-efficiency urban amphitheatre, offering a flexible sloping landscape for daily leisure. This adaptable design can also accommodate a wide range of public activities, including cultural and commercial events. The silos serve as the backdrop for the central stage, allowing visitors to connect with the historical memory of the site.

大成麪粉
铁人麪粉

To preserve the original industrial memory, we have protectively transformed the silos and plants, incorporating geometric incisions to add spatial mass where needed. This activates the original industrial space, making it adaptable to multiple functions.

The entire area is connected by the multi-level ramp park, integrating commercial events, cultural activities, and entertainment through these layered systems. Moreover, we created an industrialized "energy forest" to supply energy, a hanging bar and coastal platform offering multi-level sea view experiences, and smart units that form an urban furniture system that providing convenience for future functional changes. The open, continuous public landscape system balances "looking at" and "being looked at," allowing citizens to freely participate in shaping the spatial environment.

PROPOSAL OF JÜRGEN MAYER H. ARCHITECTS

The master plan for the Dacheng Flour Factory Project proposes an urban park. The New Culture Campus at Dacheng Industrial Heritage Project is a dynamic and lively urban park as a center for creative industries and urban lifestyle experience.

A combination of Arts, Culture, Offices, Artist Studios, Shopping, Sports Facilities, Cafés and Restaurant are set within an urban park for relaxation, events, cultural production and leisure activities. A mix of cultural and economic programs will provide economic balance and success in a self contained environment. The Culture Campus becomes an important hotspot for an international community inside the urban development of Shekou that invites people to celebrate the city and its natural setting between the mountains and the sea.

Based on a sensitive transformation of the historic site into a lively contemporary urban place the historic buildings will be kept as original as possible. The curvilinear geometry of the silos is the landmark of the site and will be used as a generator for the additional new buildings on the site, bridging the past and the future. The theme can be seen as a continuation of the historic program of the site, from Silos to Cloud – both a storage system for ideas and culture: metaphorically a storing system for culture and economy, for goods, for data and to generate communication and discourse.

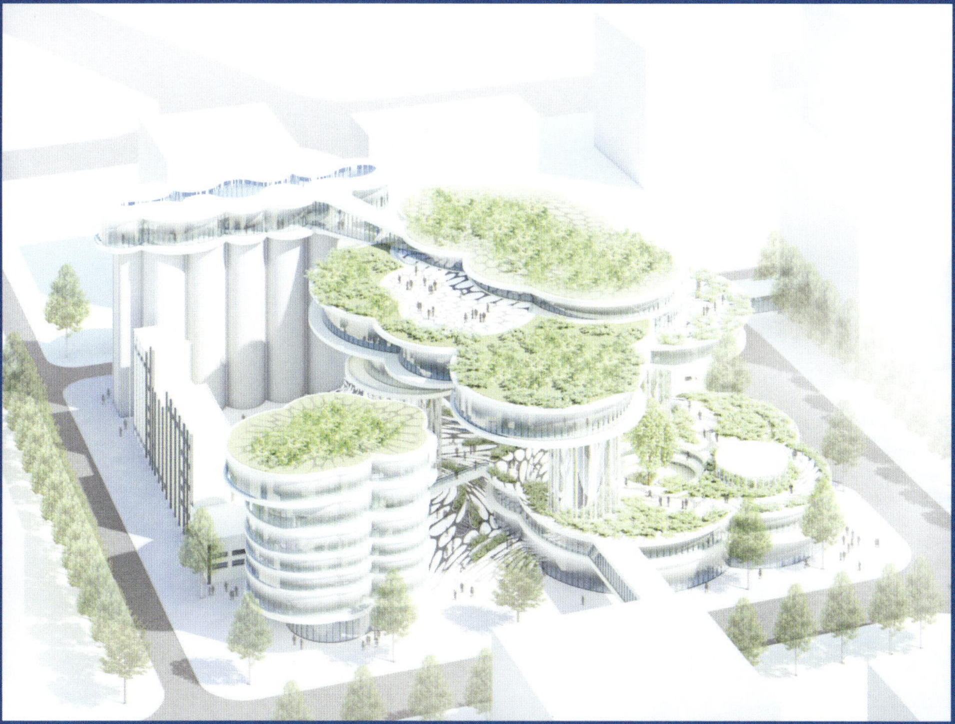

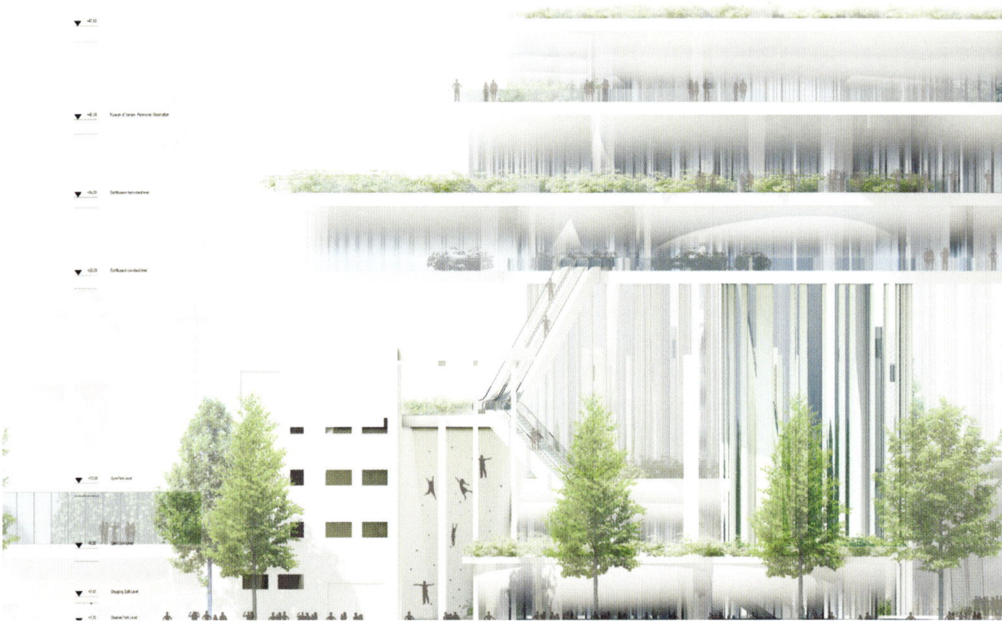

Culture Campus for Creative Industries Museum, galleries, street art and sports activities, shoppingand experience, café and gastronomy, organic healthy food market and restaurants – all within an urban park on many levels. The open spaces between the buildings provide cosy places of retreat and lively areas for activities for the community and culture. It is a vertical park as a mixing chamber for art, culture, sports, commercial areas and lifestyle activities.
The Pocket Parks between the buildings offer an informal and lively space for retreat. The Sandwich Park between the lower and top buildings will become a vertical garden on many levels. Water will be an important feature for the outdoor areas for good climate and atmospheric stimulation. The canal located underground will be echoed on the ground level by water pools and fountains.

Museums include the Art and Ecology Museum in the Cloud and the Museum of Senses in the Silos. Historic buildings include a mix of creative industry

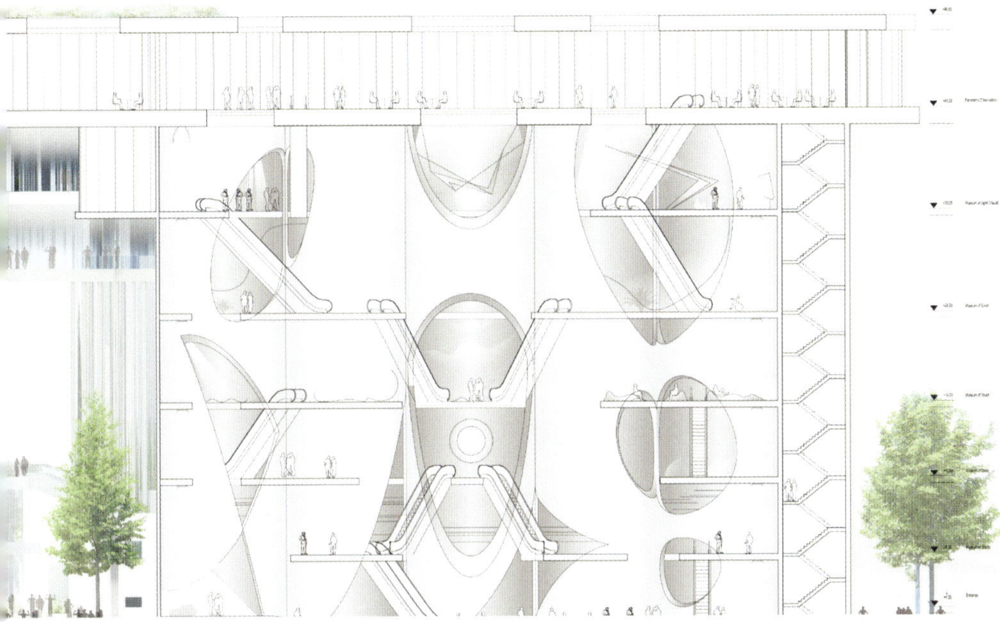

programs are placed inside the existing buildings like Hotel / Boarding House / Organic Food Court / Artist studios / Creative Laboratories. An elevated office building will define the south corner towards the harbor. Shopping, lifestyle activities and street culture experience will be located on the west corner of the master plan towards the main street and access from public transportation.

PROPOSAL OF OFFICE OF RYUE NISHIZAWA

Situated in the east-southern part of Nantou Peninsula of Shenzhen City, the Shekou Industrial Zone faces Shenzhen Bay to the east and the Pearl River to the west. The zone belongs to Nanshan District, which is the city's largest residential region and is yet blessed with mountains, lakes, and a 42 km coastline dotted with islands. The area's natural beauty is too precious to harm. We therefore propose a "green park" design that emphasizes harmony with the environment and the public.

The proposal involves construction of four towers at unoccupied spaces and installation of a sunshade covering the whole site. The design will integrate the new structures with old ones, Shenzhen's industrial heritage, and will create a large, ground-level public space that can be used for multiple purposes. We will select a sunshade with a louvered roof to let in the light and generate a pathway for rains, winds, and heat. Under the roof, subtropical grasses will be planted; planting is considered effective for building a low-carbon society. We are also planning to make a canal within the site by bringing water from the sea via old drainage lines.

As for the tower facades, we will employ aluminum expanded metal sunscreens and double-skin curtain walls with an aim to controlling air-conditioning load and thus reducing the energy burden of the buildings.

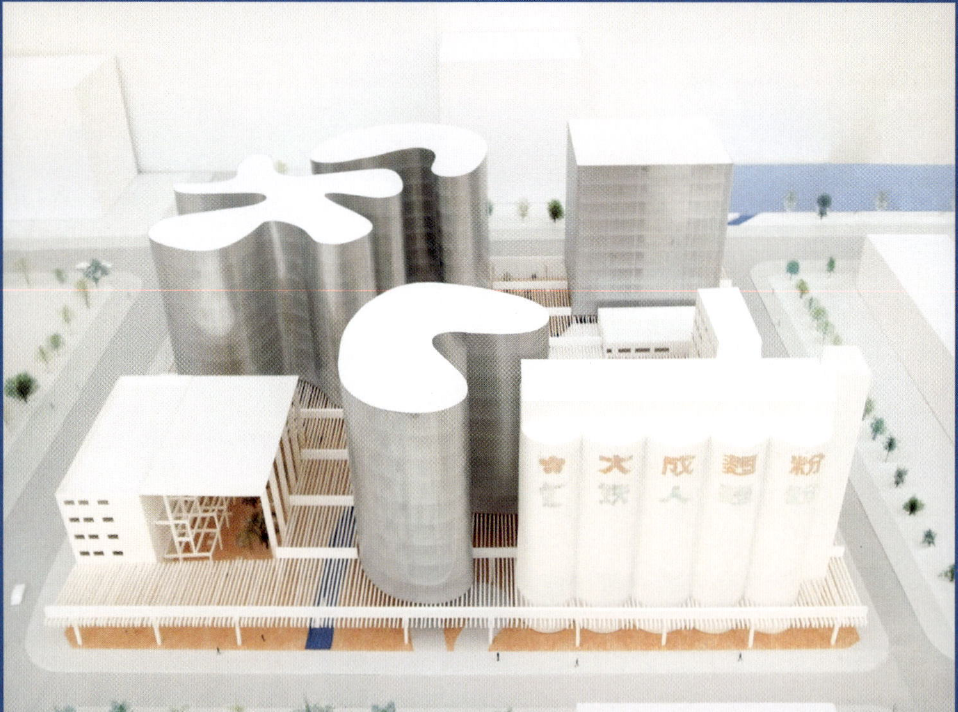
大成麵粉

The project, upon completion, will feature offices, museums, hotels, and restaurants, but visitors will not be limited to those who have a particular purpose for coming. The accessible park-like setting with green and water will also attract many of those who have no particular reason to come but just want to have a refreshing stroll, such as commuters on their way home.

We are envisioning it to look like a public garden open to the local community, and we believe our design will transform the zone into a lively but comforting and safe spot where people of all ages, whether alone or in groups, can relax, enjoy, and mingle.

III. RENOVATION

A utopian experiment at Shenzhen Speed

In March 2015, Dacheng Flour Factory was selected as the main venue of the 6th UABB. The renovation and design of the venue were entrusted to Doreen Heng LIU with NODE Architecture & Urbanism (NODE). The entire renovation project was completed with remarkable efficiency and was delivered for use in November of the same year.

Transcending its exhibition purpose, the renovation project encompassed a multitude of social ideals. A utopian community was constructed on top of the original industrial heritage, opening up the once-enclosed factory space to the greatest extent. This endeavor also forged new connections between the revitalized area, the city, and the public. By employing an approach of space reproduction, the former industrial production relations were profoundly transformed into fresh social and cultural relations. This catalyzed the emergence of new production methods and spatial arrangements, and fostered a more diverse and vibrant community life that combines the old and the new. Embracing the concept of "harmony in diversity," buildings of varied forms and functions engaged in interaction and dialogues.

CONSTRUCTION

In preparation for UABB, the construction of the Dacheng Flour Factory operated around the clock. Through the process, each building gradually transformed in anticipation of the grand exhibition event.

SANY
SANY

PLAN FOR SHEKOU'S FUTURE: RENOVATION OF DACHENG FLOUR FACTORY – 2015 UABB VENUE PLANNING & ARCHITECTURAL DESIGN

2015

Doreen Heng LIU + NODE
Architecture & Urbanism

Dacheng Flour Factory in Shekou is a historical memorial for the people in Shenzhen. Being selected as the main venue for 2015 UABB in Shenzhen, this industrial legacy will be re-activated and brought to life again through a renovation design by NODE. The renovation process was motivated not only by the practical needs of hosting the Biennale, but also by a commitment to articulate the cultural memory of the site and open the possibilities for the future. While the factory was originally designed to produce physical commodities, the renovation seeks to re-produce the site itself as a place of public life.

大成麵粉

01

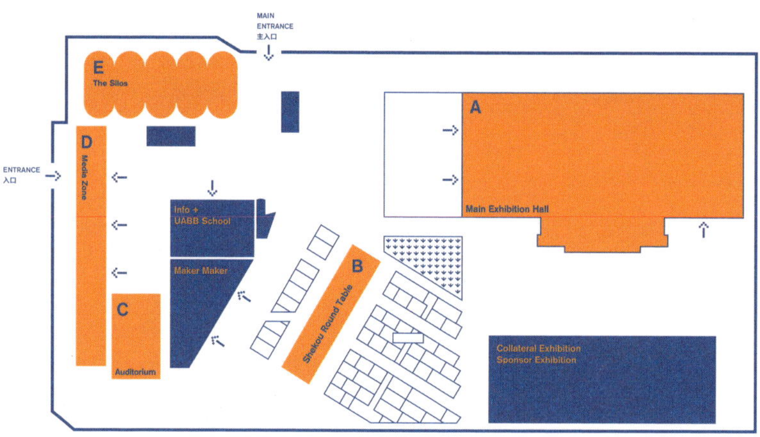

A Building #8
B Building #3
C Auditorium
D The Mill Building
E The Silos

The Five main buildings in the renovated Dacheng Flour Factory complex include:

(A) Building #8: Originally a port warehouse of China Merchants Group, this enormous classical industrial building, with reinforced concrete girderless slab, undergoes a transformation to become the primary exhibition venue after renovation. (B) Building #3: Once a simple frame-structured building, it turns into a multifunctional small complex featuring an implanted "urban kitchen," realizing a complete chain from agricultural production to the kitchen. (C) Auditorium: Lofted above an older building, the new auditorium,

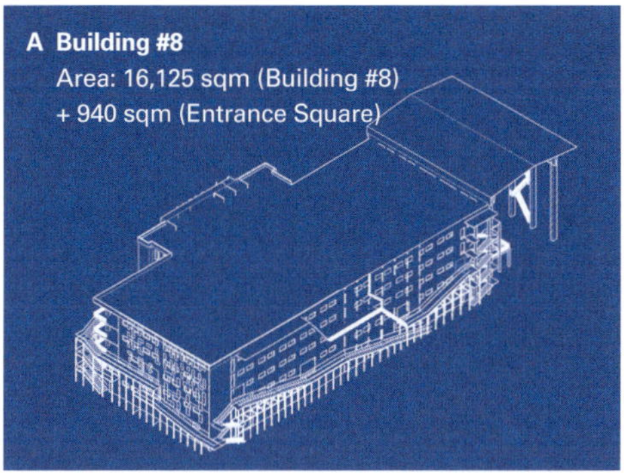

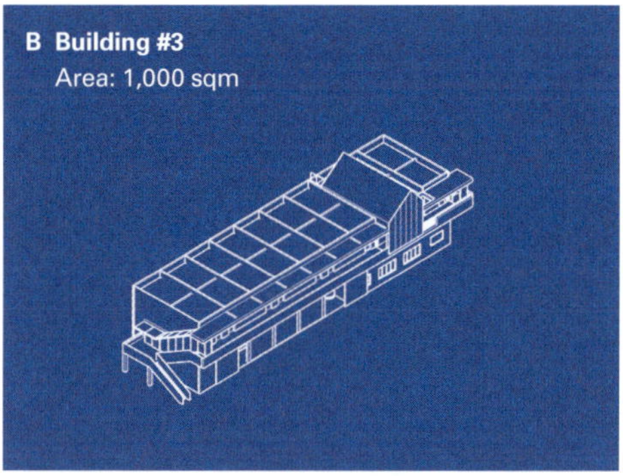

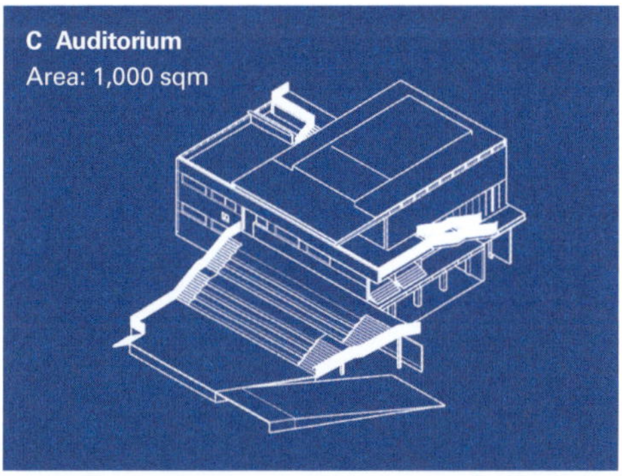

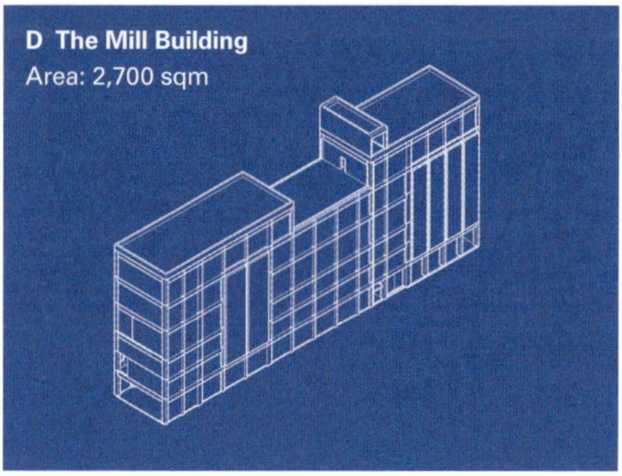

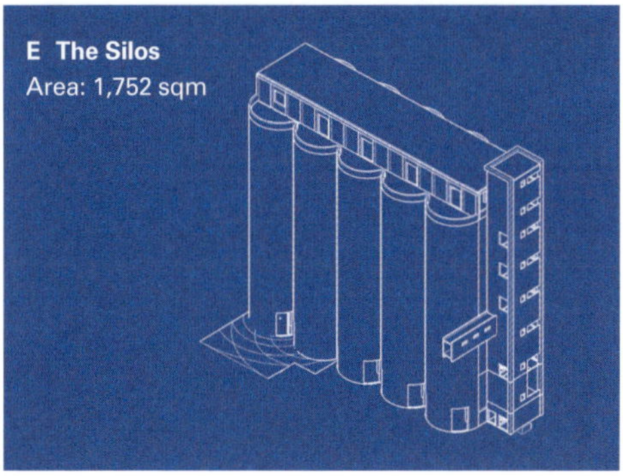

characterized by openness and lightness, offers a sweeping view of both the bay to the south and the Silos to the north. (D) The Mill Building: Through minimal design interventions, the mill building invites visitors to explore its rich space and industrial history. (E) Silos: A unique visitor circulation is created inside the iconic Silos, providing diverse and overwhelming spiritual experiences within this industrial legacy.

01 Top view of the renovated Dacheng Flour Factory Complex

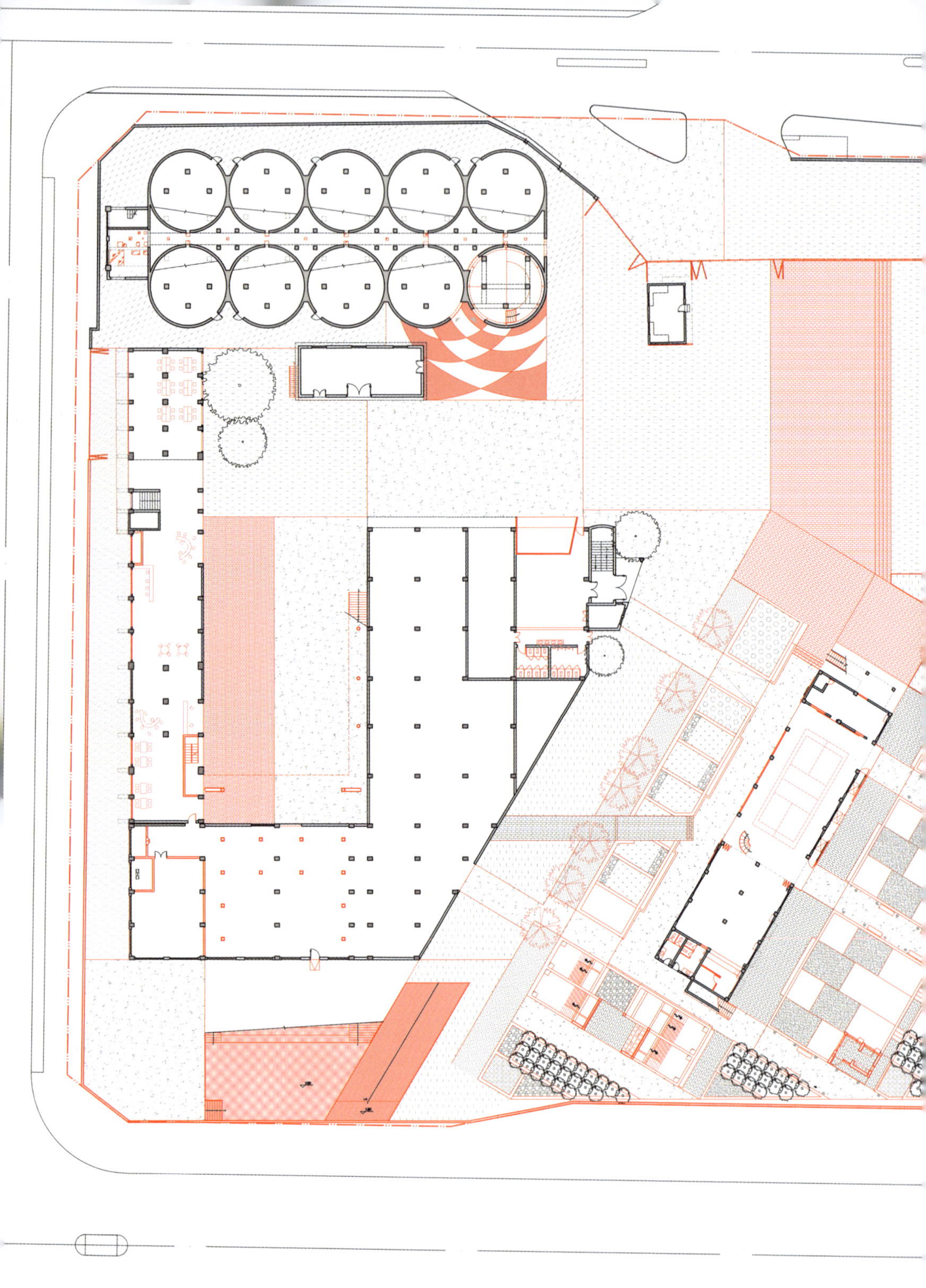

Ground floor plan of the Dacheng Flour Factory Complex

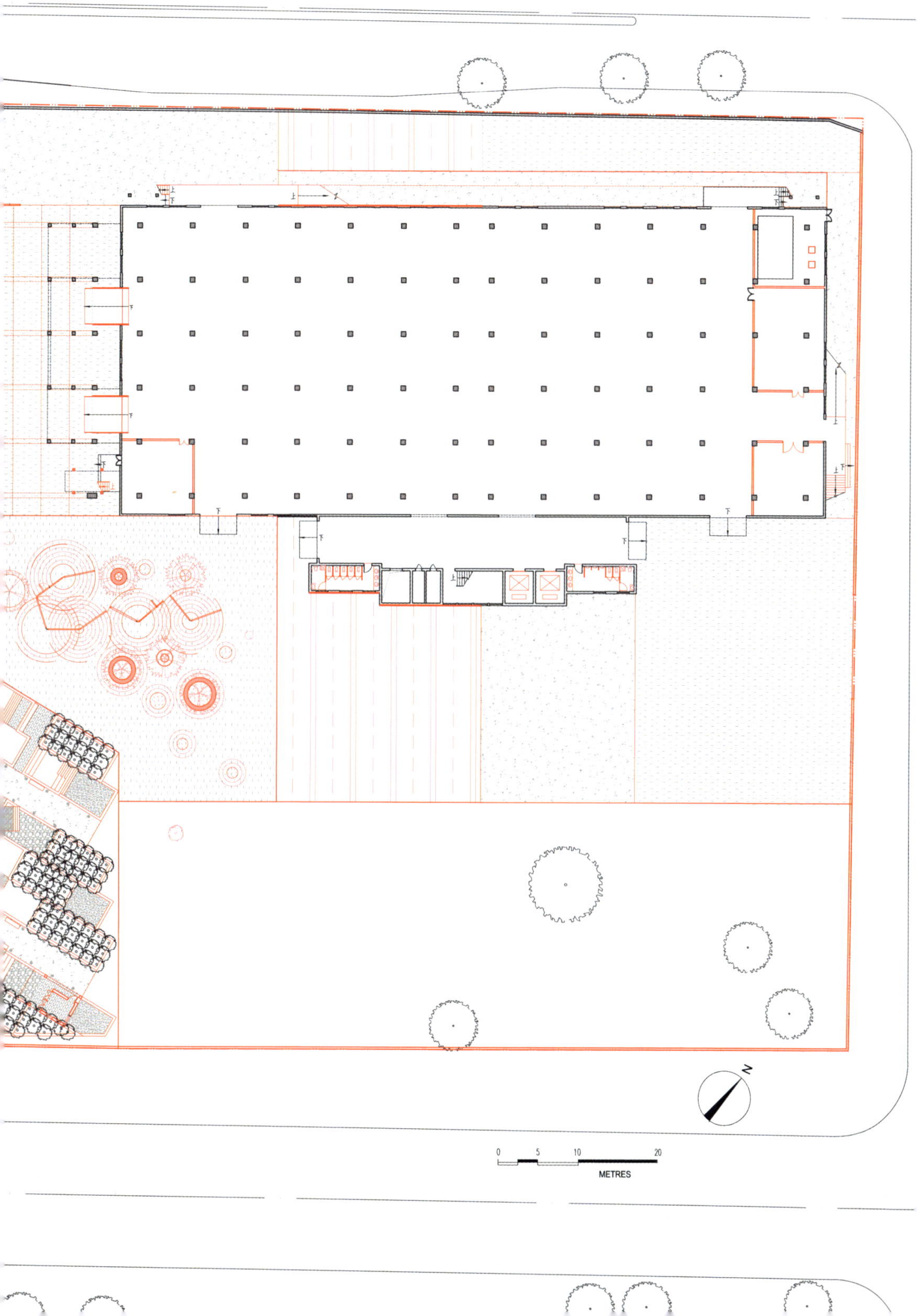
N
0
5
10
20
METRES

Building #8

Area: 16,125 sqm (Building #8) + 940 sqm (Entrance Square)

Structure: Preserving the Classical Framework

The existing warehouse #8 (Building #8) is a classical industrial building with reinforced concrete girderless slabs, a structure that is seldom found today when new building technologies emerge one after another. The elegance of the structure is overwhelming, so the original framework is basically kept untouched, except that the interior space is re-planned for exhibition to serve as UABB's main venue.

01

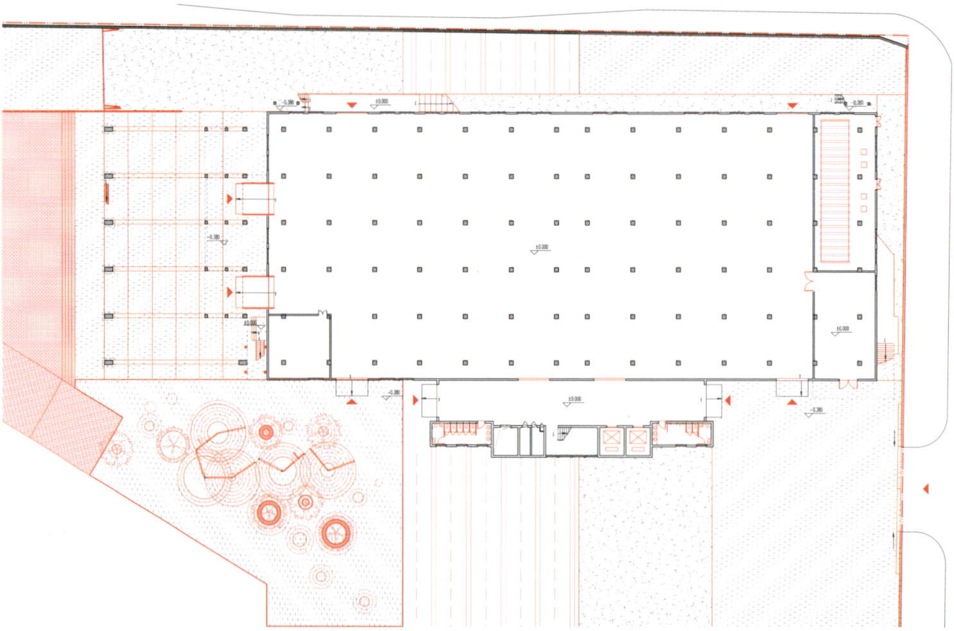

02

03

01 The original reinforced concrete structure is exceptionally elegant, requiring minimal design intervention beyond upgrading the fire protection and lighting systems. The spacious interior, once used for storing grain and goods, is now prepared to showcase creative exhibition pieces. 02 Ground floor plan of Building #8
03 The staircases under the restored canopy on the west elevation connects to the overall circulation of the building, creating multiple paths of exploration.

Façade Renovation:
Visualizing Conflict between Future and Present

In the future blueprint, a grand boulevard is to cut through Building #8. As a critical gesture to visualize such conflict between the future and the present, that future road is collaged onto the façade. Meanwhile, as the space is renovated from storage into exhibition space, escape stairs have to be added to comply with the design codes. The design amplifies the elements of "stair ramps" to extreme, to create a continuous and complete visitor circulation on the façade along the city's trunk road. This on one hand complies with the fire protection requirements, on the other hand creates impressive, dynamic and diverse façade out of the otherwise mediocre and monotonous impression.

01

02

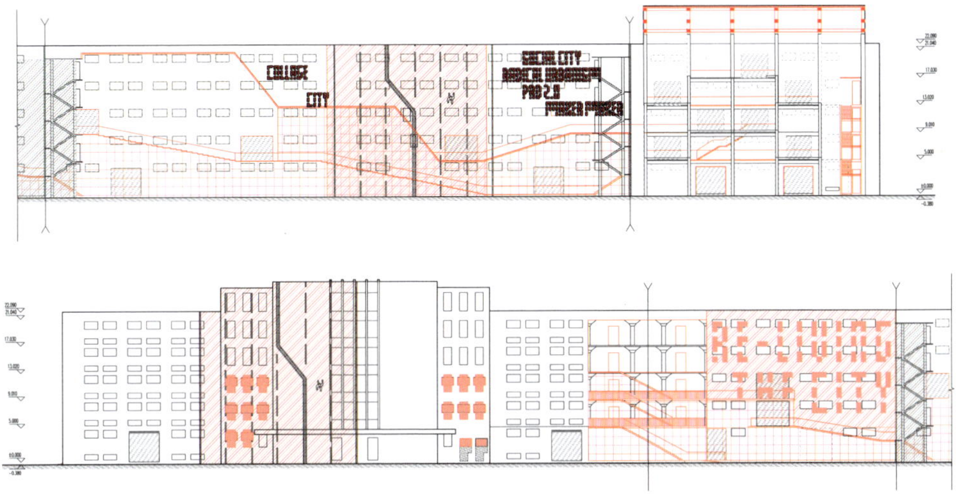

03

04

01 South elevation of the renovated Building #8: the wall graphics was inspired by the planned road through the site. 02 East elevation of the renovated Building #8: a portion of the exterior walls were removed to reveal the interior framework. 03 North and south elevation of Building #8 showcasing the wall graphics and the external circulation system around the building. 04 North and east elevation of the renovated Building #8 at night.

01

02

01 On the west side of the building, the original steel roof frame and canopy has been restored, recreates the ambiance reminiscent of the operational days of Building #8 in the entrance square. 02 View of the Building #8 from the street 03 The restored roof frame and canopy 04 Ground floor entrance

Entrance: Restoring the Roof

The entrance to the whole renovation project is placed at the southwest side of Building #8, where an empty cement structure used to stand. The main effort here is to restore the former steel roof frame and recreate the status and scene when Building #8 was in operation, thus re-shape the sense of place on the entrance square.

At schematic phase, highly-reflective mirroring materials were proposed for the roofing of the structure as a gesture to invite the surrounding landscaping into the square. Unfortunately the architect's attempt to interpret the past and the present of the industrial legacy within one site was not actually realized due to the pressing construction schedule.

03

04

After UABB: An Alternative Scheme for Building #8

NODE also proposed a plan to integrate the previously planned road through Building #8, with the dual purpose of preserving the historic structure and facilitating the future road connection to the cruise homeport. The strategy involves the removal of the ground and first floors of Building #8 along the path of the road, while reinforcing the remaining structure to maintain the building's stability. This approach strikes a balance between urban traffic needs and architectural preservation while also offering a unique experiential space.

01 Rendering of the alternative scheme for Building #8 02 Section and elevation of the alternative scheme to let the road pass through the building

01

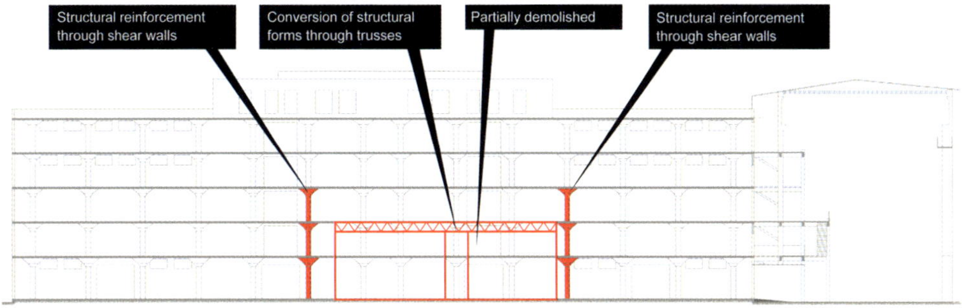
Structural reinforcement through shear walls
Conversion of structural forms through trusses
Partially demolished
Structural reinforcement through shear walls
02

Building #3

Area: 1,000 sqm

Combination of Tangible and Intangible: Interplay of Functionality and Space

Building #3 seems to be a quite ordinary frame-structured building with few distinguishing features on the site. Yet beneath this mediocre shell there lies a diverse possibility of spatial combination inside. To cope with the existing conditions and pay tributes to the quality and old spatial combination, various new functions are implanted here.

01

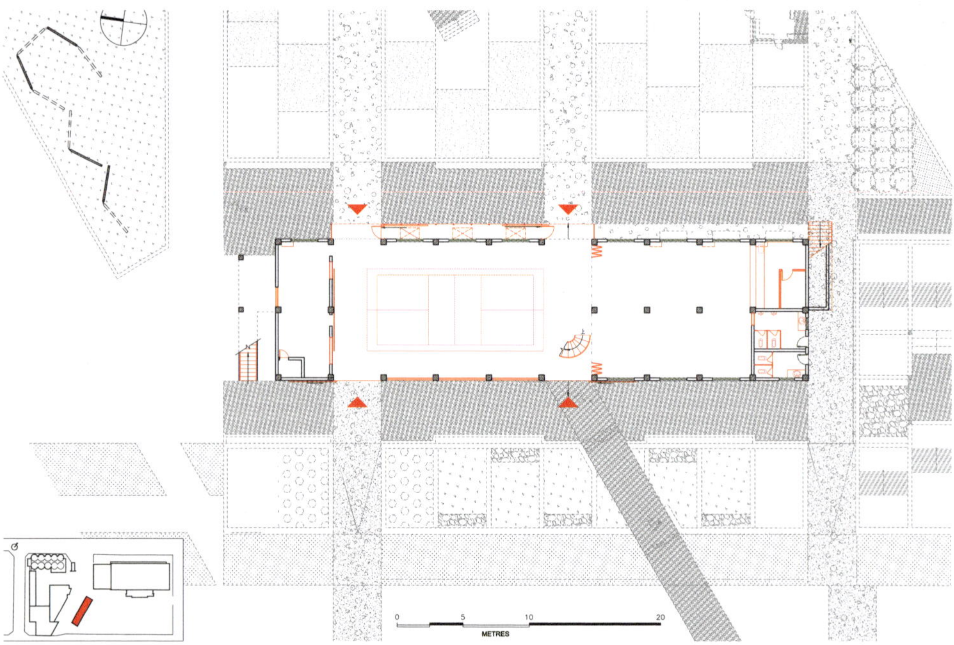

02

03

04

01 East elevation of the renovated Building #3 02 Ground floor plan of Building #3 03 West elevation of the renovated Building #3 04 East and west elevation of Building #3

The generous space on the GF serves as the education hall and concurrently badminton court. GF and 1F in the south accommodate the cafeteria and offices. On 2F, the linear relationship with the former employee dorm is reserved and the youth hostel is planned. Shared kitchen and laundry rooms in the middle energize the singular accommodation function and create an activity center on this floor. Finally a garden farm is placed on the rooftop. Such an organic combination of the overall functionality with the space contributes to a micro complex for public education.

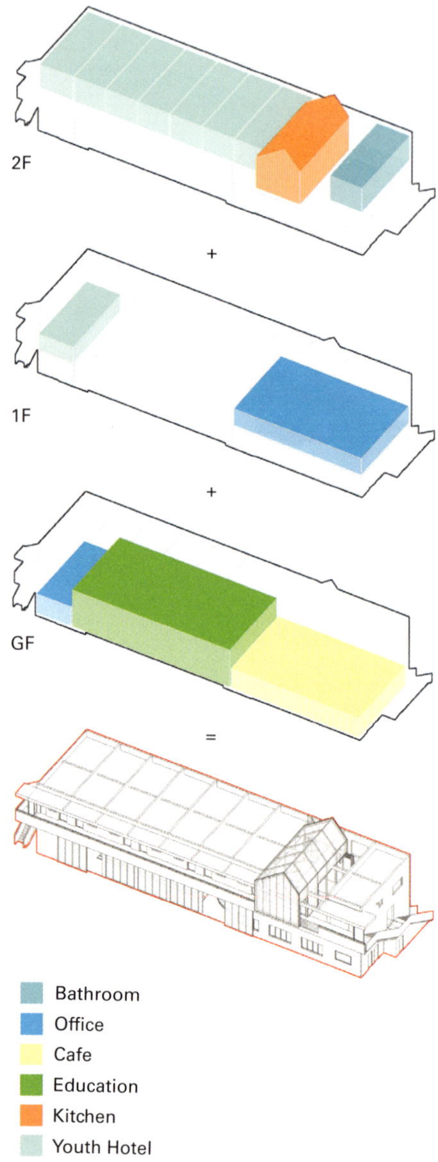

01

01 Isometric diagram of the renovated Building #3, demonstrating the diverse and vibrant mix of functions.
02 After renovation, the spacious first floor features high-performance self-leveling floors and flexible furniture, and can be alternatively used as a public education space or a badminton court.

02

Experiment of Urban Kitchen:
An Ideal Mini Community

To change the mediocre look of the whole building, a slope-roofed small house is inserted into 2F as a highlight. This small house accommodates an "Urban Kitchen" that serves the urban dwellers and their informal interaction, and shapes up the sense of place and belongings in this mini-community.

While keeping the original building frame to the maximum, efforts are made to realize the urbanism ideal implied by Urban Kitchen, i.e. to create a mixed-use small complex and provoke the rethinking over the fast-growing industry and cities.

To respond to the concept, a landscape designer is invited to conduct the agriculturally-themed landscape design, i.e. "Floating Fields", around Building #3. The interplay of the architecture and landscaping calls for return of agricultural mindset, i.e. harmony of nature and human, above the industrial relic left over from the drastic development of Shekou, and re-examines the relation among people, society and nature.

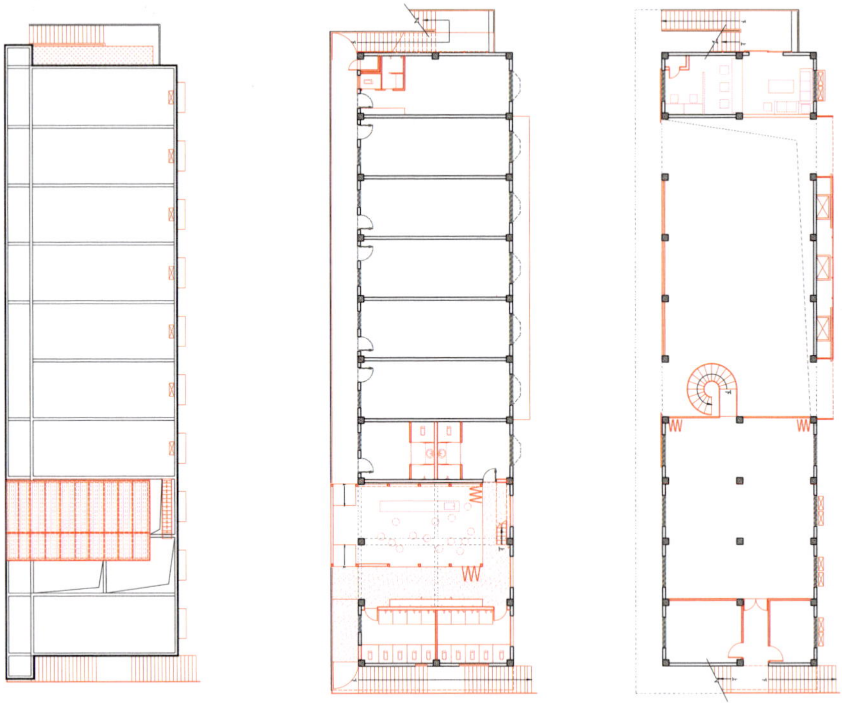

01

01 Floor plan of Building #3 02 The transparent Urban Kitchen space implanted on the third floor can serve as an informal meeting and exhibition space during the biennale. 03 The space of Urban Kitchen changed the mediocre look of the whole building. 04 The agriculturally-themed landscape, Floating Fields surrounding Building #3, draws inspiration from the traditional "mulberry dike-fish pond" agricultural model in the Pearl River Delta. 05 Diverse crops are cultivated in the Floating Fields.

02

03

04

05

Auditorium

Area: 1,000 sqm

01

Auditorium as Viewfinder: Maximizing Landscaping Resources

A new auditorium is lofted above an older building. In the north of the site stand the Silos which, with the highly sculptural volume and impressive height, boast the most distinctive feature of Dacheng Flour Factory; while to the south of the site there unfolds the fantastic sea view of the busy Prince Bay. So how to invite both views into the renovation and make them part of the attributes of site becomes the starting point in the design of the Auditorium. As response, visual corridors and some height points are provided in the north and south of the site to avoid the sense of enclosure caused by the box-like industrial building. The north and south façades are defined as two gigantic frame finders to bring in the most attractive views, meanwhile, create an open and transparent performance space against the urban backdrop. With addition to and renovation of the Auditorium, GF is featuring the Maker Maker exhibition, 1F includes bathrooms and meeting rooms under the steps, and 2F is equipped with a leisure terrace. Furthermore, the spaces of the Mill Building are borrowed to serve as VIP lounge. With interplay and organic combination of the functionality and space, a mini-conference complex is created.

02

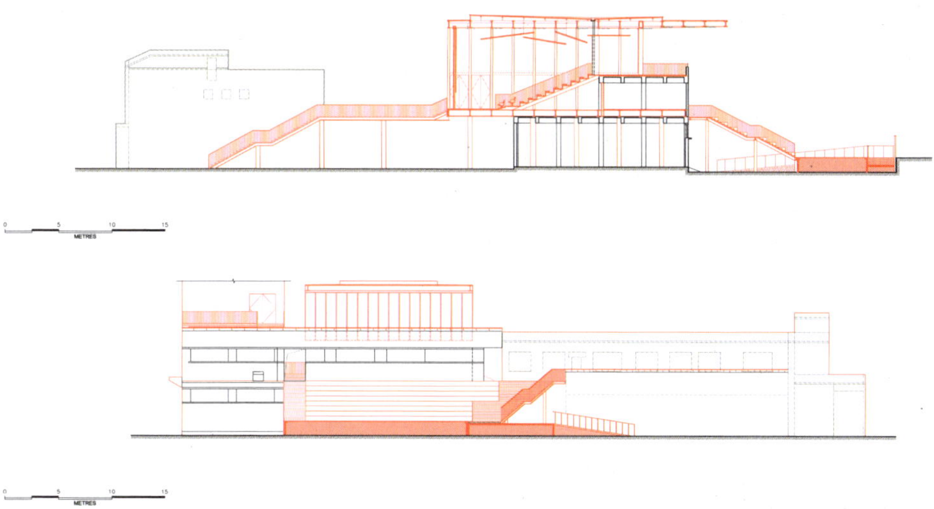

03

01 The Auditorium provides a panoramic view of the sea and the surroundings. 02 The renovated Auditorium is endowed with multiple functions: it can serve as an observation deck, a semi-open versatile grey space, or as a practical interface for public activities. 03 Section and south elevation of the Auditorium

01

02

Contrasting Volumes:
A Dialogue between the Old and the New

The renovation here still follows the principle to "adapt to and give full play to the existing conditions and maximize the reuse of objects." The original building here is also a typical factory building without much distinctive features. As typical column grid cannot accommodate the use demands of the large span space for the Auditorium, half of the column grid on 1F is removed to create a platform on which the new structure is gently placed. This enhances the contrast between the new and old volumes, and between the two eras, restoring to the maximum the rethinking of design on the fast-growing industrial development.

Separated from the old building, the new structure, a door-type steel frame, appears like a glass box gently placed on the half-grid platform on 1F of the old building. The contrast between the new and the old is also embodied in materiality and texture. The new building volume, which is light and transparent, contrast with the solid and stable temperament of the industrial building.

Due to the extreme constraint like the construction schedule and coordination, the structural dimensions of the lecture hall do not achieve the desired lightness. Yet this can still be regarded as a bold experiment.

03

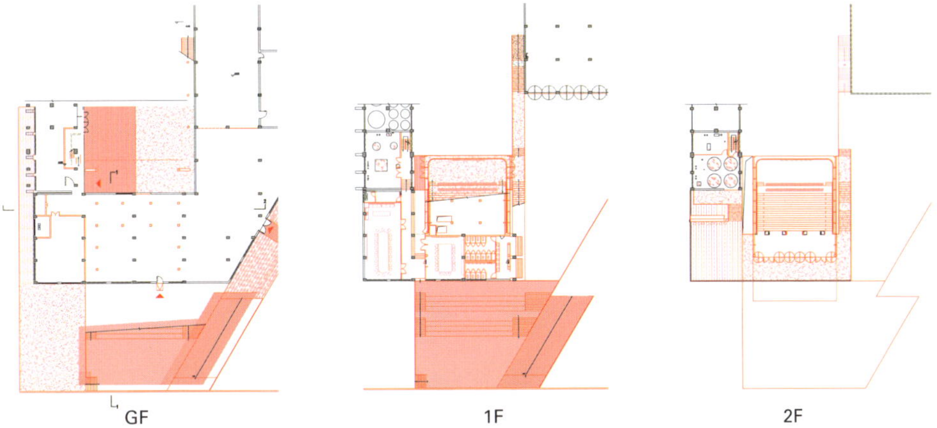

04

01 The operable interface between interior and exterior 02 The bright and spacious hall 03 Steel columns penetrate the old structure, providing essential support for the new Auditorium. 04 Floor plan of the Auditorium

The Mill Building

Area: 2,700 sqm

01

Reshaping the Industrial Memory: An Encounter with Production Line

The mill building is a spatial embodiment of the whole flour processing workflow, directly responds to the intricacies of the process technology, reflecting the logical connection between the form of industrial buildings and their functions. In the renovation of the mill building, we adhere to the same logic and principle by integrating new functions into the respective processing spaces and establishing a new flow line. Just a few design moves, including selected cut-outs through the slab and the addition of new staircases, allow visitors to access the rich space and industrial memory within.

02

03

01 After the large grinding machines were removed, numerous holes in different shapes were left inside the building, creating an unusual spectacle. 02 These holes are either retained or filled with glass or steel frames to maximize the sense of permeable space and the original appearance of the industrial heritage. 03 The ground floor is opened to the public to the maximum extent. 04 Section of the Mill Building

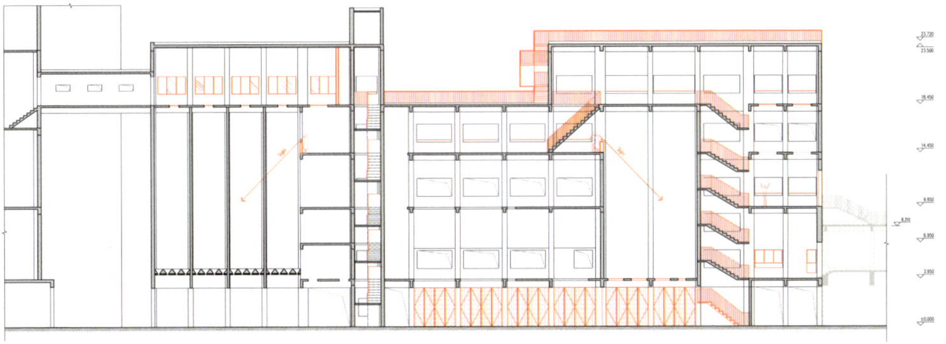

04

The Silos

Area: 1,752 sqm

NATURE
MACHINE HALL
VALUE FACTORY
S&O
Bi-CITY BiENNALE

01

02

The Landmark: Emphasizing Authentic Spatial Attributes

The Silos of Dacheng Flour Factory have been used for storage of grains in this flour "empire." The ten massive cylindrical silos still rise and the eight Chinese characters saying "Dacheng Flour" and "Ironman Flour" on the top edge still remain visible after witnessing the ups and downs of the factory and even the industrial development of the whole Shekou Industrial Zone in the past decades.

01 The design aims to preserve the inherent attributes of the Silos, accentuating the essence of time, space, and texture within it. 02 A distinctive visitor pathway navigates through the second floor of the ten silos, where varied lighting generates distinct atmospheres in each space. 03 Gazing upwards inside the Silos, one is enveloped by the the immense volume and coarse qualities of the industrial space, enhanced by echoes, resulting in an extraordinary experience. 04 Plans of the Silos

03

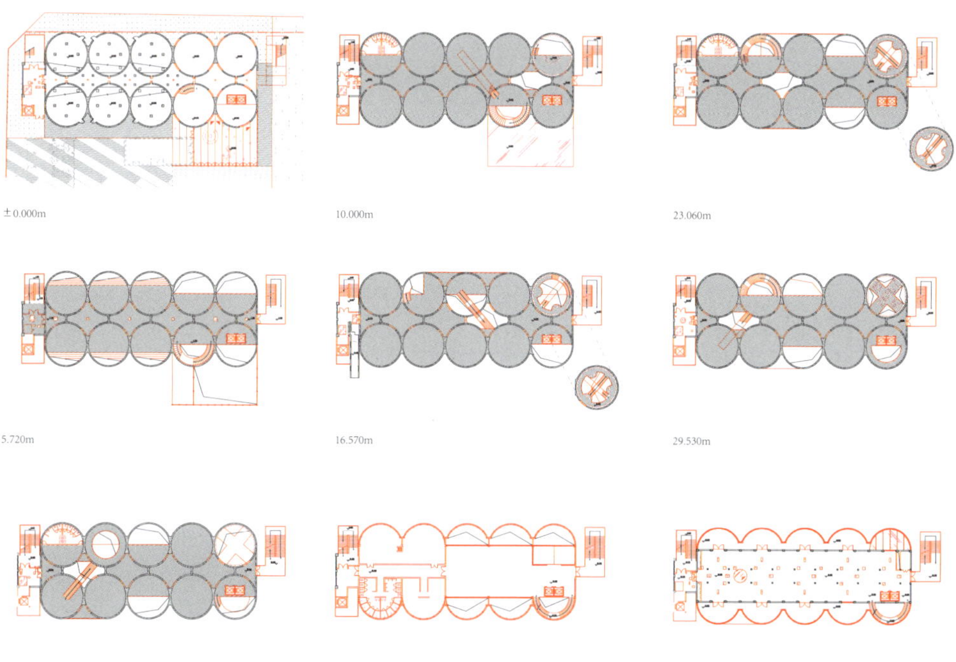
±0.000m
10.000m
23.060m
5.720m
16.570m
29.530m
35.500m
46.400m
40.150m

04

Undoubtedly, the Silos are the most unique and important structures on-site. As their original functionality has become less critical, the design focuses on preserving and restoring the authentic spatial attributes of this industrial building, maintaining its solid appearance and emphasizing the internal experience of time, space, and texture. A unique visitor circulation is created inside the ten silos. Each silo uses different lighting to foster different atmosphere and create diverse and overwhelming spiritual experiences.

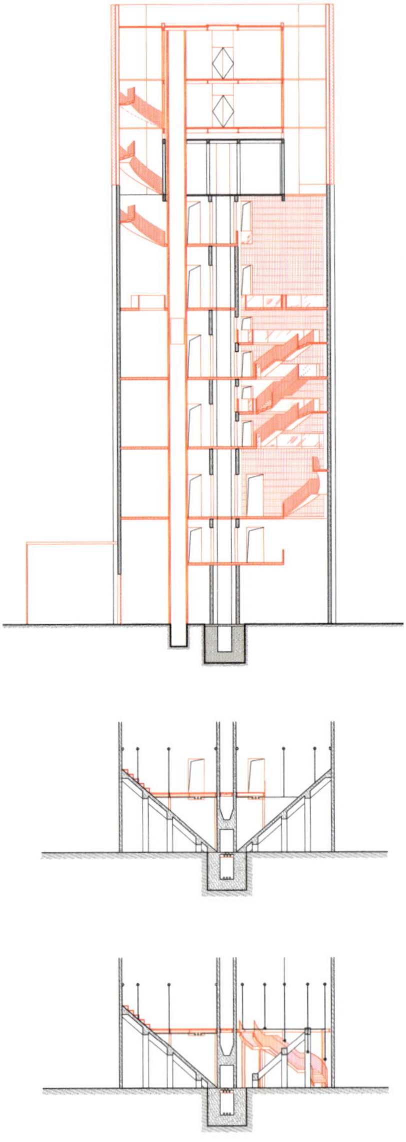

01

02

03

01 Sections of the Silos 02 The ground floor of the Silos, originally designated for loading and transporting food ingredients, remains unaltered. Additional lighting has been introduced to the long corridor to encourage exploration and evoke the imagination of past production activities. 03 The cuts in the walls connect each independent space of the Silos. 04 The pathway cut through the walls of each adjacent silo, guiding the visitors to walk through the magnificent industrial legacy. 05 A silo space that can be used for meditation or small screening events.

04

05

01

02

Future of the Silos

The renovation plan for the Silos for cultural use is expected to continue after 2015 UABB. The main silo spaces are planned as an art museum, where a continuous central steel stair will be implanted in a center-to-center manner in the ten silos to connect the spaces on different floors and establish the main visiting circulation. Meanwhile, libraries and full-height meditation rooms are placed now and then along the way to highlight the spiritual attributes of the Silos and elevate the visiting experience to a new level. The top floor of the Silos will follow the cloud-like profile to create more transparent volumes featuring office spaces.

03

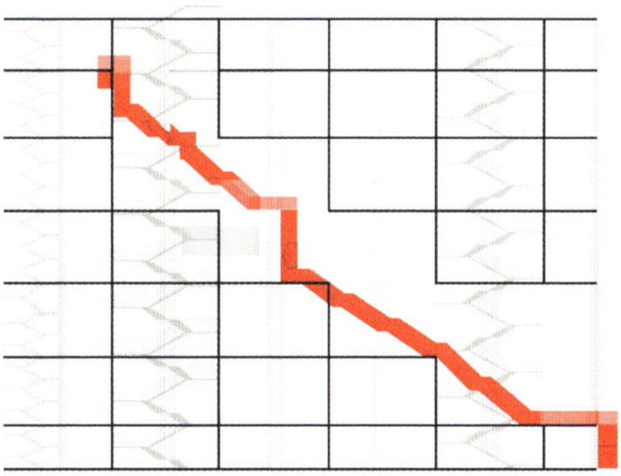

04

01 Various functional spaces, including a library and a meditation room, are planned along the way to enhance the spiritual attributes of the space. 02 The main space in the Silos will serve as a contemporary art museum, featuring a continuous steel staircase implanted at the core of the ten silos to establish the visitor circulation. 03 Envisioned Future: The uppermost floor of the Silos will undergo transformation into office space, complementing the cloud-like silhouette with the addition of transparent volumes. 04 Circulation diagram of the Silos

IV. BIENNALE

Reproduction and transformation of space

As the 6th Bi-City Biennale of Urbanism\Architecture in Shenzhen opened, Dacheng Flour Factory experienced a profound transformation from a site dedicated to food production to a hub for cultural production. Under the theme "Re-living the City," this edition of UABB was curated by Aaron BETSKY, Alfredo BRILLEMBOURG, Hubert KLUMPNER and Doreen Heng LIU, advocated the reuse, rethinking, and reimagination of architecture and the prevailing conditions of the city. The renovation of the Dacheng Flour Factory was meticulously conducted, taking into account the city's original aspirations, local conditions, and the optimal utilization of materials, aligning seamlessly with the theme of the exhibition.

The exhibition garnered widespread attention of international and domestic audience. Over the course of three months, more than 100 works from 25 countries and regions were showcased, accompanied by a remarkable lineup of over 200 public events. Dacheng Flour Factory welcomed over 250,000 visitors from around the world, who were immersed in the distinctive power of industrial architecture and ambiance of the era. The factory received accolades in prominent media coverage, being hailed as "a revitalized new cultural landmark of the city."

DURING UABB

On December 4, 2015, the biennale officially opened. The side of the Auditorium facing the Silos opened up and became the main stage for the opening ceremony.

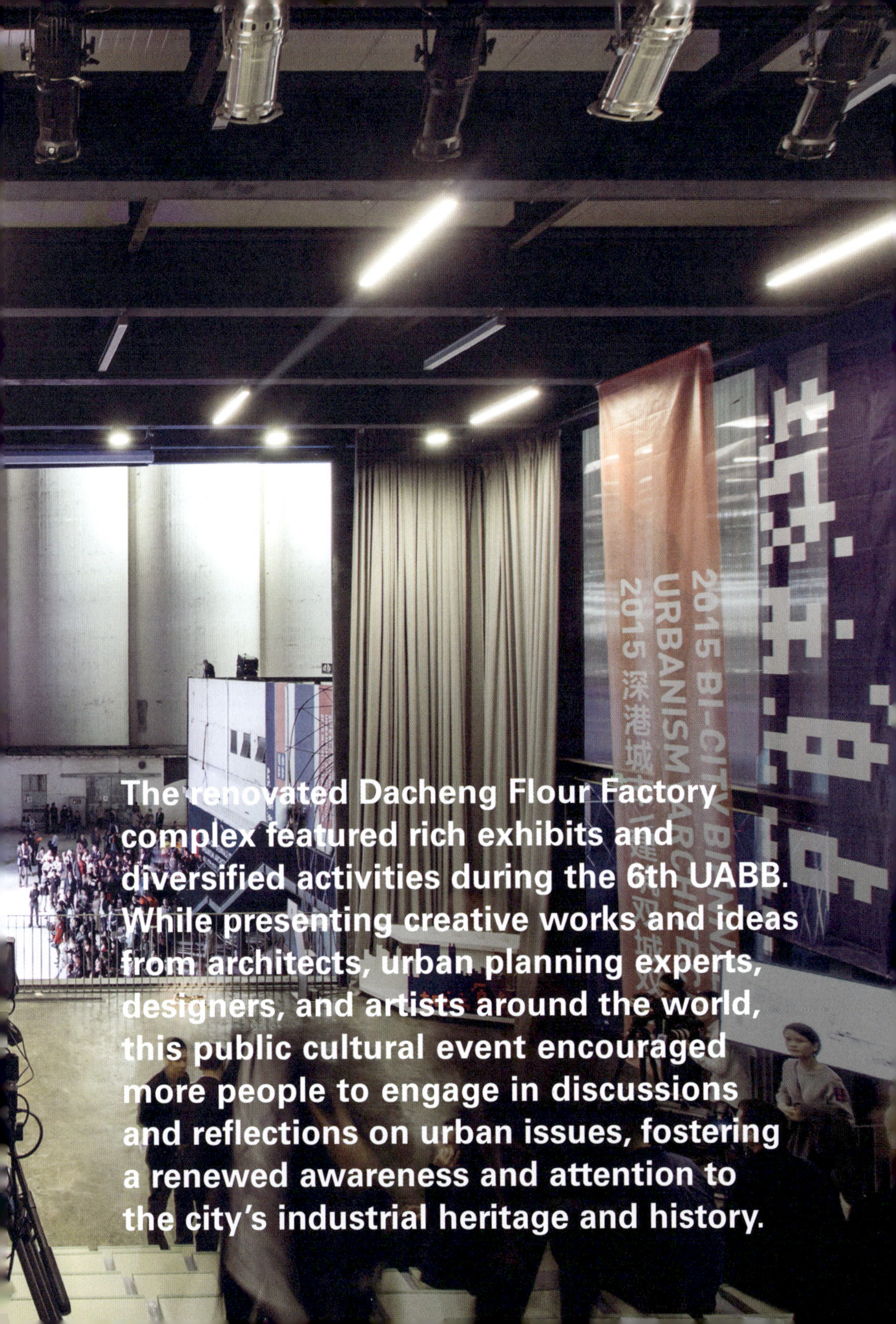

The renovated Dacheng Flour Factory complex featured rich exhibits and diversified activities during the 6th UABB. While presenting creative works and ideas from architects, urban planning experts, designers, and artists around the world, this public cultural event encouraged more people to engage in discussions and reflections on urban issues, fostering a renewed awareness and attention to the city's industrial heritage and history.

01

02

03

01 The opening ceremony featured a captivating multimedia projection performance, specifically tailored for the Silos. It artfully illustrated the industrial history and the envisioned future of both the factory and the city. 02 The keynote forum of the "PRD 2.0" section took place in the Auditorium. Over the course of the biennale, numerous forums, workshops, roundtable meetings and other events unfolded at Dacheng Flour Factory, fostering an open environment for public participation, communication, and discussions. 03 The chief curators welcomed both domestic and international media representatives in front of Building #8, offering insights into the content of the exhibition and the highlights of the renovation project.

PRINCE BAY
嘉宾
VIP
签到处
SIGN
政务
签到处
SIGN
公众
PUBLIC
签到处
S GN

RE
RE-LIVING
THE CITY
城市原点

Transformed into the primary exhibition space, Building #8 displayed works with extraordinary ideas on urbanism and architecture across its three floors, including three main sections: "Collage City 3D," "Radical Urbanism" and "PRD 2.0," along with the special program "Social City."

AUTONOMY &
AUTODIGESTION

The surroundings of Building #3 became a favored leisure spot for visitors. Hydroponic crops flourished in the floating fields, and ducks leisurely swam. Internally, Building #3 hosted the Shekou Industrial Zone's thematic exhibition, "Shekou Roundtable: 2025," and also functioned as an event space. Numerous themed roundtable forums deliberated on the shared future of Shekou during the biennale.

01

02

03

01 During Christmas and New Year, a vibrant creative market event took place in the square in front of the Silos. Designers, artists, illustrators, bakers and craftsmen from various cities set up stalls, drawing a crowd of customers across different age groups. 02 A forum on space and light took place on the second-floor podium adjacent to the Auditorium. The Silos' iconic presence during the night is enhanced by the carefully positioned lighting that highlights the structure. 03 A small architectural animation screening was hosted by exhibitor Liam Young within the Silos. The dim ambiance and the echoing surroundings crafted a unique and immersive experience for the audiences.

DACHENG FLOUR FACTORY: THE UNDERLYING LOGIC IN VALUATION OF INDUSTRIAL HERITAGE

Interview with ZHANG Yuxing

ZHANG Yuxing, one of the major founders, organizers and facilitators of Bi-City Biennale of Urbanism\ Architecture (UABB), Chairman of UABB Academic Committee, President of Shenzhen Biennale Foundation, Researcher of the School of Architecture and Urban Planning of Shenzhen University (Deputy Director of Benyuan Design Research Center), Founder and principal architect of ARCity Office.

ZHANG served as the Division Chief for Urban and Architectural Design/Deputy Chief Planner of Urban Planning, Land & Resources Commission of Shenzhen Municipality from 2009 to 2016, and the Director of UABB Organizing Committee Secretariat Office for four editions from 2009 to 2015.

Date: 22nd June, 2022
Place: Online Interview
Interviewers: Doreen Heng LIU, LIU Si
Editors: LIU Si, LI Sen

Factory as the Exhibition Venue

Why we made Dacheng Flour Factory the main venue of 2015 UABB had something to do with the Float Glass Factory, one of the main venues of 2013 UABB. From 2005 to 2011, UABB were held at either OCT-LOFT in Nanshan District or Shenzhen Civil Center in Futian District. In 2013, the Organizing Committee confirmed the theme of UABB that year was "Urban Border," a challenging topic, that requires a proper venue to echo this theme.

As we all know, Shenzhen has its urban borders on the west, east and north. The west border in Shekou enjoys relatively convenient traffic conditions and we thought perhaps we could find a suitable venue there. So we contacted China Merchants Group (CMG). ZHENG Yulong, the General Manager of Planning and Land Development from CMG Shekou Industrial Zone, was in charge of such issues. He then took us around to different locations that may potentially serve as UABB venue, and we finally selected the Float Glass Factory and the old Shekou Ferry Terminal. This means we first visited Dacheng Flour Factory during the preparation for 2013 UABB, and the whole process of site selection of 2015 UABB was a natural extension from the previous edition.

Dacheng Flour Factory stood beside the road on our way to the Float Glass Factory. Drive about 300 meters west from Shekou Ferry Terminal, and you would see the silos, the most striking structure of the Flour Factory from the road; and, the Float Glass Factory is just one kilometer ahead. Dacheng Flour Factory was actually located between the two main venues for 2013 UABB.

It has always been the tradition of UABB to discover a place, then revitalize it, and transform it into a truly meaningful urban location or even a district to exert a wider range of influence. Moreover, as the 2013 UABB was well received by the public and academia, and considering that the terminal area of Prince Bay was less developed and much ignored by the public, we decided to hold another UABB in Shekou, where many industrial heritage resources were located. The Flour Factory had better transportation than the Float Glass Factory and possessed well-preserved industrial heritage, including a complete flour production line of silos, mill and workshops, so naturally it became the main venue for 2015 UABB.

We already knew the planning of the Prince Bay area when we were selecting UABB venues, and, as per the regulatory detailed plan at the time, one of the main buildings (Building #8) in the Flour Factory area would be demolished for the proposed boulevard towards the new cruise homeport. So why did we still select the Flour Factory as the main venue? It's because we were thinking whether it possible to partially change the plan via UABB, such as re-mapping the road network or providing an underpass. If this was not possible, at least we could keep the Silos and the Mill Building. It was out of such consideration that CMG agreed to hold UABB there first, and then see what to do next depending on the actual situation.

After the Flour Factory was selected as the main venue, we had discussions with CMG, trying to make some changes to the plan, for instance, opening up the basement of the Building #8 to allow for the underpass while retaining the upper two floors. Both parties made efforts, but for various reasons involving a whole set of land planning processes, approval and policy issues, the building was torn down in the end. To be fair, CMG should not be blamed for this. After all, the urban planning preceded UABB and this outcome was somewhat inevitable.

Unfortunately, the preserved Silos and the Mill building fail to extend the value of the UABB. However, the life cycle of industrial heritage is actually very long. I also believe that the current owner will attach great importance to these heritage buildings. In fact, they have had several editions of plans developed to tackle issues like development and operation.

It will take some time before Dacheng Flour Factory can be truly transformed into a value space in the city.

Consolidate the Value of Heritage

The Silos and the Mill building are included into *The List for Protected Historical Buildings in Shenzhen (The Second Batch)*, which was undoubtedly facilitated by the UABB. Since the Float Glass Factory was turned into an exhibition venue, people began to realize the value of industrial heritage; and even before the list was released, these two facilities had been regarded as industrial heritage. During the UABB, we already started to think about preparing a list for Shenzhen's heritage buildings, especially the industrial heritage sites. Immediately after the closing of UABB, we started to work on the classification of the list and these two factories were included. This is a naturally extended process.

To transform the factory buildings into heritage and consolidate the value of heritage through UABB, consensus had to be made with CMG. Theoretically, CMG could have demolished all these buildings, since no restrictions were specified in the plan or contract when the land was allocated. Yet CMG generously lent these facilities for UABB exhibitions and events, which fully demonstrated their awareness of the value of heritage and the willingness to make efforts. The preservation of the Silos and the Mill Building in the end was actually facilitated jointly by the government, enterprises, and the public. This is, in my opinion, where the value of UABB lies: It discovers places or heritage sites in the city that have not been noticed previously, and then transforms them into social consensus through exhibitions, and exert some impact back on their owners. Generally speaking, once a place is turned into the main venue of UABB, people would realize its value and then actively protect it.

The UABB Mechanism

The value of UABB lies in its close connection with the city. UABB is different from the Venice Biennale or other biennales in the world that held at permanent venues. Though these biennales also discuss urban issues, they are actually disassociated from the cities and do not really throw themselves into the real urban life, not to mention identifying problems through on-site exhibitions, solving problems once detecting them, or turning problems into new urban values. That's why UABB is an innovation even in the global biennale system. You may notice that some Chinese or foreign cities have drawn inspiration from UABB – the Shanghai Urban Space Art Season is a typical example. This innovative combination of "urban curation" and "urban site" is a complete system. It is no longer restricted within the main exhibition venue, but instead, intervenes into the city gradually for synchronized development. Such a strategy, or action, has received widespread attention.

UABB's venue is more of a concept, idea or methodology than just a specific location. As UABBs held at OCT-LOFT, Nantou Old Town, and the Float Glass Factory turned out to be very successful, people become more convinced about UABB as a methodology. People may notice that the government and developers, especially large developers, are particularly interested in UABB; and right after the closing of the event, would quickly intervene in the development of the venue. In this way, a virtuous circle is formed, and people begin to understand the impact of UABB and the possibilities it offers. Enterprises also recognize the value behind, such as activating the venue, attracting more visitors, and gaining trust from the government. The market is very sensitive to the dynamics, and the moves of the enterprises indicate not only social and cultural value, but also economic value behind. Things that cannot bring economic value would be difficult to sustain, no matter how they have been acclaimed.

The Value of Industrial Heritage

In early days when we didn't see any value in industrial heritage, we refer to it as "industrial remains," which sounds less significant than heritage. In terms of reuse, most of the time they are reused as functional spaces, because they have large spaces and relatively complete structures. They can be transformed into creative parks or office buildings, or reused for many other purposes. However, this leads to a new misconception. Because they can be easily used for so many purposes, we tend to focus on functionalities while ignore the core value elements of industrial heritage. This is, in my opinion, a common problem encountered in the current protection and regeneration of industrial heritage in China.

Now that the area around Dacheng Flour Factory had been highly urbanized, it would undergo quick, drastic depreciation if we just simply turned it into a small creative park, office facility or exhibition venue, as the spaces available are limited. Given such a situation, I believe we should weaken and even eliminate the functionality of the Flour Factory in the future, and make it a purposeless or multi-purpose space, a space of pure emptiness, before any enhancement or remolding efforts could be made. Only in this way can industrial heritage acquire a new spiritual attribute or public value. This is actually a process of recreating industrial heritage. It does not simply preserve or reuse the original industrial heritage, but instead, is a process of remodeling. Without such remolding, the industrial heritage can never be differentiated from the highly urbanized surrounding areas, nor the core value of the heritage be properly appreciated. What we see is just an old building of minimal value.

The areas around the Float Glass Factory were relatively underdeveloped, which helped generate an internal tension between the industrial heritage and modern life style. Yet this same approach would no longer work for Dacheng Flour Factory, as its surrounding areas had thoroughly changed. Turning the Flour Factory it into a creative industrial park or similar facility, in my opinion, would greatly reduce its value. I personally believe that a new heritage regeneration strategy should be adopted for the Flour Factory to appreciate its true value.

The Revaluation of Space

Not only industrial heritage, but heritage in our daily life also faces this problem. In the early days, the concept about heritage was simple, that was to reuse it. On one hand, people regarded it a waste of land if the buildings were not properly reused; on the other hand, they reject any proposal to really demolish these buildings. In terms of reuse, a new problem also emerged compared with the value of the land, the spatial value of the heritage is minimal, as you can neither tear it down, nor expand the floor spaces. Consequently, developers, the government and architects all felt being trapped and misled, and neither demolition nor reuse, as simple solution, would really work.

I think this involves the core value of a heritage. Nowadays, how should the spatial heritage be revaluated to serve the society? Revaluation does not mean to add value, but to highlight the core value of the heritage itself and incorporate it into a larger value cycle. Only by doing so can such projects become appealing to developers and government. We need to consider how spaces regenerate value in the new social system, rather than merely emphasizing the cultural attributes of heritage. Cultural heritage also needs to be incorporated into life of modern society. After all, it is not a cultural relic.

So how could our heritage become part of a large cycle within a new economic system that involves real estate, land and economics? Retaining a heritage, means transferring the spatial value to an adjacent location to compensate for the owner's loss. This way, an internal value cycle is formed between the two, and the value gained in the adjacent location can be injected back into the conservation of the heritage.

The Western countries have developed a sophisticated mechanism for heritage protection through the transfer of spatial value. However, they also face challenges and this mechanism has not seen wide implementation. But I think that we should be able to fully practice this mechanism when massive urban regeneration get started in China. Once such a value cycle is realized and the problem of land value is addressed, the government and developers will be fully motivated to work on heritage issues. After all, heritage revitalization and protection can bring positive influence on their own brand building and business operation. This is a more realistic approach in China at the moment. We are now promoting this idea to the government, hoping to identify the value of heritage within a slightly larger system, including the interaction of the heritage with the land economy of the entire city. This approach can tackle issues relating to heritage protection, and meanwhile enabling developers to gain rewards for the protection of heritage.

As for Dacheng Flour Factory, technically it's feasible for the owner to increase tens of thousands of square meters in the Prince Bay project, but whether to do it or not is a issue of mindset, specifically, whether the government is willing to accommodate the increase of plot ratio. If people think that the heritage of the Flour Factory is deemed very important, the government can approve corresponding floor area to be developed by the developer at a nearby location, which is a benefit for the developer and will in turn supports the heritage protection and revitalization. The city can increase tens of thousands of floor area without any harm. So why not just put it into practice? Because our own system limits the production of such value.

Through such a straightforward bundling and balancing process, the problems encountered in urban heritage protection can be solved. Relying solely on the outdated, limited system would lead to a dead end where removal becomes the only option. In reality, we can see many successful cases response effectively to land planning policies and mechanisms.

The industrial heritage issues are not totally resolved in Western countries, but I think there is a chance for China to work this out. Public ownership of land in China facilitates balancing land use on a broader scale. China has potential to integrate heritage into a larger economic cycle, establish a theoretical system based on practices, and then promote such theories to influence others. Once the planning and administration departments realize the feasibility of such approach, technical operations can be efficiently managed behind the scenes. So as architects and planners, we should serve to call more attention to this new possibility.

V. OUR FAILURE

The disappearing heterogeneity

Following the conclusion of the 6th UABB, several buildings within the renovated area of the Dacheng Flour Factory were inevitably subjected to the unfortunate fate of demolition. Amidst the currents of urban regeneration, this industrial heritage, which was as old as Shenzhen Special Economic Zone, once again retreated into silence, awaiting an unpredictable future.

UABB's strategy of activating the grey areas as a catalyst through exhibition represents a pioneering urban experiment. It embodies a development vision that focuses on diversity, inclusiveness, and striking a balance between the old and the new. However, as each edition of the exhibition comes to an end and the fervor wanes, the practical challenges and key contradictions of urban regeneration once again resurfaces. How to sustain positive influence, balance cultural values, and achieve the sustainable operation of the venue is evidently the long-term challenge that must confront to truly achieve its "activation."

This is the atypical journey of the flour factory thus far and also serves as a testament to the ever-evolving dynamics and games in the era. While "Shenzhen speed" has shaped this remarkable city, in the fast-paced and ever-changing yet homogenized urban life, how much richness and heterogeneous vitality have we forfeited?

DEMOLITION

Building #8, conceived as an architectural manifesto responding to the theme "Re-living the City" of the 2015 UABB, rapidly succumbed to an accelerated "De-living" shortly after the exhibition. In August 2016, when Building #8 reappeared in the media's lens, it was already in ruins. Torn down after its "rebirth," the building's fate garnered significant attention and sighs. By the end of 2019, Building #3 and the Auditorium in the renovated Dacheng Flour Factory area were also successively demolished.

RE
RE
RE-LIVING THE CITY

SANY

禁止跨越

MADE IN SOUTH CHINA
南中国制造

Interview with Doreen Heng LIU

Doreen Heng LIU, Founder and Principal Architect of NODE Architecture & Urbanism, Distinguished Professor of Shenzhen University, Director of the Greater Bay Area Innovation Design Lab.

LIU served as one of the chief curators of the 6th Bi-City Biennale of Urbanism\ Architecture (UABB) in 2015, and led the planning & architectural renovation project of the Dacheng Flour Factory.

Date: 5th April, 2023
Place: NODE Architecture & Urbanism Shenzhen Office
Interviewers: ARTDBL (ZHONG Gang, XI Tong)
Editor: XI Tong

In 2015, Shekou started a new round of development and scheduled, in the development plan for Prince Bay, the first road connection to the new port. Dacheng Flour Factory happened to be sited on the planned road, so it was decided to demolish the factory. However, it was also in the same year that the Flour Factory was selected as the main venue for UABB with the theme of "Re-living the City."

UABB's pioneering experiment to "activate" urban areas has been underway for 18 years, equivalent to the time it takes for a child to grow up. During this period, we have seen UABB's pioneering efforts in discussing urban issues, and its achievements in transforming existing areas by drawing on its own experimental advantages. At the same time, we cannot ignore the many regrets that UABB faced, such as Dacheng Flour Factory's difficulty in keeping up with the rapid pace of renovation in the old Shekou district, and the demolition in less than a year after completion of a series of design renovations.

Doreen Heng LIU said, "Our experience with that edition of UABB was absolutely a tragedy." Dacheng Flour Factory's fate begs the question: are cultural and historical values really not important to this city? Eight years have passed since "Shekou Relaunch." Today when we look back again at this part of the city which has been covered by other facilities, we might as well ask, what kind of creation has it witnessed and how much history have we lost?

Dropping a Pebble in Water

ARTDBL: The value of which UABB is most proud is the activation of grey areas in the city, but after you completed the renovation and curation work at Dacheng Flour Factory in Shekou in 2015, Shekou's Prince Bay project advanced rapidly, and most of the old factory areas you proposed to preserve have been demolished. Eight years and three UABBs later, in what new light do you now see the "affinity" between UABB and this city via such activation?

Doreen Heng LIU: UABB has made indelible achievements, and indeed opened up an era. The value of the biennale itself is to advocate experimentation and the avant-garde, which represent the possibility of new space production in this city. When discussing experiments, space transformation, and "activation," however, in the final analysis, UABB is not an entity responsible for continuation. What is most critical is that, it is the entity that truly performs the "activation" and its demand for benefits, as well as its interactive relationship with the biennale and the government, that ultimately determine the survival of the space. Previous editions of UABB, moreover, did not offer so many direct utilitarian benefits. The funding came from various sources. Little by little, money was collected and invested in the preparation of the exhibition, so the investors wouldn't interfere in what exactly the exhibition did. When a biennale is dominated by a single fund, however, the questions of "who is endorsing" and "for whom" will arise.

The 2015 edition, for which we did a lot of work, from software to hardware, featured a high degree of internationalization and substantial diversity in content. We also conducted extensive research related to UABB's pioneering position on urban issues, and put forward many feasible ideas regarding critical urban issues, but the exhibition venue still could not escape the fate of demolition. Take Nantou Old Town, the venue of 2017 UABB as an example, after seeing that this place had aroused public attention, the relevant parties carried out commercial transformation very keenly. The follow-up operators of Dacheng Flour Factory, however, didn't prioritize the public attention generated by the event or the venue's cultural value.

The demolition of an industrial site may not seem that important in the city's development, but it suggests a future direction. Is this direction progressive or regressive? When renovating Dacheng Flour Factory, we opened the first floor to the community, but after the biennale, it closed again. Why was the planning so aggressive, and with what purpose?

Therefore, we had to revisit the UABB exhibition venues, and conduct a discussion based on space production in the entire city of Shenzhen: have we really fulfilled the objective of activation?

ARTDBL: Moving around the city without a permanent exhibition venue in a nomadic strategy, UABB carries with it a new mission in each edition, to activate spaces one by one. This is pretty like carrying an "explosive package" to blow up a "bridge", a very heavy mission in itself. The legitimacy of UABB seems to lie in the fact that it works, and that it is a useful "activation kit."

Doreen Heng LIU: The biennale is actually now caught in a predicament. You may be right about the role of the "explosive package." Anyway, it's like carrying a bomb to blow something up. The biennale just provokes an issue, regardless of the consequences, to initiate the action of "explosion." When the curtain fell on the UABB in 2015, urban villages were mentioned as the direction for the next UABB venue. Instantly, like a pebble dropped into a calm pool, it stirred a thousand ripples, diverting public attention to urban villages. Similarly, Dacheng Flour Factory was also a stone that splashed the water, but everything eventually returned to normal. What had to be demolished was still demolished.

From "City, Open Door!" to date, UABB has lasted 18 years. So what are we doing now, and for what purpose? Since 2005, one of UABB's goals has been to activate the grey spaces in the city one by one, but what is the purpose of the activation and have the spaces really been activated? Considering the current trend of spatial development in Shenzhen, we cannot help asking and thinking: is it now even worse than it was in 2005?

A Dream of Power

ARTDBL: In the same year after the 2015 UABB was concluded, demolition of the Dacheng Flour Factory area began, along with land reclamation and new area development. I believe that 2015 can be regarded as a turning point for Shekou. At that time, Shekou called constantly for "Shekou Relaunch," and by holding two consecutive UABBs, it seemed to be returning to the vision of public culture. After 2015, however, there were fewer and fewer discussions, and development became Shekou's main theme. This also shows that after 2015, Shekou still chose to become a development-oriented industrial zone, rather than an "experimental zone for Reform and Opening-up."

Doreen Heng LIU: In the process of China's development, Shekou, like many other places in China, cannot determine its own destiny; there is something above them. Shekou used to enjoy a highly independent existence, planning and approving for itself, making it the experimental field for Shenzhen's Reform and Opening-up. However, Shekou today has become a part of the blueprint of the Greater Bay Area and the value of experiment is diminishing. This also poses a very strong impact on the fate of Dacheng Flour Factory, which is not a place that is incapable of retaining old things, but there is a dream of power.

If Shekou wants to drive the development of the entire area, the first thing to do is to reconstruct the roads, which is why Dacheng Flour Factory was planned to be demolished in the first place. Anyway, for development purposes, the first road connection must be established, which is an inevitable "relaunch." For us, however, the meaning of relaunch is not to develop more homogeneous new districts, but to implant another kind of experimental production while retaining the industrial heritage. In both the 2013 and 2015 UABBs, we hoped to replace the large-scale demolition and construction with the transformation of the entire old factory building area in Shekou and thereby drive a new business model, but, in terms of results, we failed.

It is very interesting to put Dacheng Flour Factory and Prince Bay together. The purpose of the former is to activate the community, while that of the latter is a capitalist process of accumulation. This site represents two different values. As a result, the community lost to capital. They won, and we lost. Put simply, that's the way it is.

ARTDBL: Also, it was some time after 2015 that Shekou's development direction became an important aspect of the Greater Bay Area. Your studio was formerly in Nansha, where you did a lot of design experiments and research. In your view, what is the conceptual difference between "the Pearl River Delta Region" and "the Greater Bay Area?"

Doreen Heng LIU: There is always an administrative intent behind the change of name. The Pearl River Delta Region is first of all an ecosphere that includes animals, plants, nature and the human environment. It is a concept of geography and the humanities, while the Greater Bay Area is an administrative concept with objectives. The Pearl River Delta is a regional concept, while the Greater Bay Area is a strategic component, which involves many different factors. They carry extremely different meanings.

ARTDBL: More than 20 years ago, Rem Koolhaas conducted a series of studies on the Pearl River Delta. Do you think that set of discussion frameworks is still applicable in the context of the Greater Bay Area?

Doreen Heng LIU: What Koolhaas saw at the time was that, in this socialist city, there were some embryonic forms of mature capitalist cities. This must have been very exciting for architects, because, with the construction of Shenzhen and the Pearl River Delta just started, there were many opportunities. Shenzhen at that time was very similar to the West in the first half of the nineteenth century. It enjoyed, for example, the earth-shaking changes brought about by new technologies and developed a lot of infrastructure.

His observation regarding the development of Shenzhen was generic city (ordinary city), namely all cities and villages of the same appearance, maximizing efficiency by crushing all heterogeneity. If we look, for example, at the fate of Dacheng Flour Factory, it is also the result of heterogeneity crushed by efficiency, so Koolhaas's summary from that time is still applicable today.

Heterogeneity

ARTDBL: When we describe Shenzhen's high efficiency, it actually means that we paid a price for it. The development of a city, for example, involves the reduction of a kind of friction. The retention of the old, for example, will affect the city's inexorable development, so the city is constantly renewing and reinstalling its system to operate at optimal speed.

Doreen Heng LIU: In fact, of all Chinese cities, Shenzhen is the one that least wishes to carry "burdens," so how the city appears to be represents such a system of values. The reason why Shenzhen has its current speed is that it does not need to pay for its past, has no burdens from the past, and its only goal is to move forward, further and further, to the forefront. Space, culture, history, life, its past... are not what Shenzhen cares, be it there or not. Several new areas developed in recent years, such as Shenzhen Bay Super Head-quarters Base, Qianhai, and Liuxiandong, do represent a possibility for the future, but are these new areas truly "new" or just following the existing routine?

I once travelled to three cities in three days, from Shanghai to Suzhou and then to Hefei, staying in new hotels in each city. Looking out of the hotel windows, I found the views outside in these three places completely the same. Then I started to doubt myself because I discovered that I myself was someone without history. I went to different cities and, although time and space changed, the views outside my windows, to my surprise, looked the same. Human space and human beings are, in a sense, one wholeness. Temporality is like an anthropological specimen. Your space represents your history, and the thickness of a city is superimposed by different time segments. So, when renovating cities, create the new within the old and preserve the historical value of the old, because your past is the most important part of your inner heart.

ARTDBL: You mentioned earlier the failure you experienced in Shekou. I think the "relaunch" emphasized in Shekou after 2015 was a process of eliminating the daily life and the organic nature of Shekou, by such means as road widening and wharf extension, and in Shekou, a new coastal area, even seas are all "tooled." Its sea-scapes, for example, are sold as commodities, and its sea routes serve as an economic resource. The "Shekou Relaunch" of that time is now rarely mentioned. Now I think we can talk, based on the exhibition practice then, about "Shekou re-examining." Such a re-examination does not mean to target at others, but it is all about examining ourselves – what is the ultimate purpose of what we do?

Doreen Heng LIU: If you look at land ownership in Shenzhen, you will find that several major real estate companies have obtained the rights to develop and use land along the coastline. Shenzhen is also a city of absolute privilege, an intensely proud "experimental product," enjoying unique policies during its construction process, and directly connected with the central government in terms of finance and taxation. Evaluating the history of the city and its form of existence from the perspective of ownership, we can understand certain core issues. The development logic behind a city is always about politics and economics, while cultural professionals always think from a culture-oriented perspective. So problems of urban development might never be solved.

Shenzhen itself is a city highly planned by the elite. This top-down planning has eliminated the vitality of everyday life. The only sense of liveliness remaining is concentrated in unplanned communities such as urban villages. If the urban villages are dismantled and the residents displaced, the last sense of everyday life will be completely gone. But the management of a city lies in the balance of differentiation. Where the mainstream exists, heterogeneity should also have its place. If management is only to eliminate heterogeneity, then what kind of management is needed? Heterogeneity should be managed in a way that preserves the diversification it represents.

It is naturally inefficient to take care of the demands and emotions of every smallest unit, but after sacrificing heterogeneity to increase efficiency, the city will inevitably face a kind of homogeneity brought about by repetition and stereotype. There used to be a slogan in Shenzhen, "Efficiency is life," but efficiency is not equal to vitality, and homogeneity cannot provide experience. Dacheng Flour Factory established a kind of heterogeneity. The sense of experience of this space comes from its particularity. Only heterogeneous things possess vitality, but this particularity is quickly crushed.

For my own architect office, I also hope it can create something from an objective and human perspective, rather than representing certain large groups. I insist, in this complex, diverse society, on trying to undertake a kind of "diversity," a different possibility, which might not follow the mainstream but has its own value of existence. There should be a reasonable place to accommodate me in society as the society should encourage for multiple voices. If differences are eliminated, people will simply become machines.

ARTDBL: We can think of Shenzhen as a city of rendering, where people are just models.

Doreen Heng LIU: Today's Shenzhen seems like a city that created with AI, because it doesn't tolerate errors. The ideal Shenzhen might be a city that can be created completely with AI, but without heterogeneity. When AI encounters uncontrollable and unquantifiable elements like Dacheng Flour Factory, humanities and history, its language pattern lacks a way to deal with such mutations. So people may be just models in an AI-generated city. Everything in an AI-generated city is legal and fair, but not necessarily reasonable. I think this may be the greatest challenge Shenzhen will face in the future.

At a Venice Biennale, Yoshiharu TSUKAMOTO studied cities in the eyes of Westerners. He dubbed the urban planning of Paris – with its radial central axis – "Monarchism," reflecting that cities under this system have such a central axis. When it comes to New York, there is no central axis. Each block is uniform, emphasizing the individualism characteristic of capitalist cities. Then, Tokyo, classified as an organic city, well accommodates daily life and shows features of the times and a bottom-up development. In Shenzhen, these three forms are all found, but which is dominant? This is what we need to discuss.

Reflection

ARTDBL: In recent years, I have noticed a trend in which architects are increasingly involved in government-led bidding for public buildings. In the past, many architects practiced independently and established offices to maintain their independence, but now they undertake more and more projects from government entities in order to survive. Do you think this is a good thing or a last resort?

Doreen Heng LIU: State-owned capital and private capital present two completely different situations for the operation of architectual programs. Private enterprises are more market-oriented and more realistic, because for every penny they spend they must get what is worth a penny, and a building that costs one million is what is worth one million. Their finalized goals are very objective. In cooperation with government or state-owned enterprises, however, the cost of labor or materials is often compressed.

A private enterprise will clearly inform the architect of what it wants, because it is itself the ultimate user. In a state-owned capital project, however, architects will have to undertake more, such as identifying problems on their own, conducting research, and drafting the design brief. As the government is not the end user, the architects are disconnected from the user from the very beginning. As a result, there are many things they fail to consider in design as to whether they are needed by the city or the citizens. Is an opera house, for example, something that this era needs? Sometimes you should think over and over again.

ARTDBL: I have noticed that Shenzhen is constantly building cultural venues, among which are the "Ten Major Cultural Facilities in Shenzhen," which have drawn great public attention. From the perspective of content operation of venues,

Shenzhen's enthusiasm lies more in the construction of facilities but lacks investments of funds and manpower for the subsequent operations, which is somewhat peculiar, a little bit like buying a horse without a saddle.

Doreen Heng LIU: Cultural buildings and facilities are ultimately for the realization of "culture," and hard-ware is ultimately the spatial carrier of software. In many instances, we very often naively pay attention to the architecture itself, but turn a blind eye to the soft power. When there are many cultural buildings in the city, will the value of culture itself truly be celebrated? We need to reflect on the more important, soft aspects over and above spatial awareness. Sometimes we see in other excellent cultural facilities around the world that, from architectural space to internal planning, everything seems to flow so smoothly from the very beginning. This is because the building itself is a space carrier for spiritual transformation, while the carrier itself depends on culture, as culture represents the soft power of architectural space.

Facing the failure of Dacheng Flour Factory, I find that our attitude towards culture and cultural architecture may need to be reweighed. The attitude, strategy, and degree of acceptance of macro policies reflected in cultural facilities and urban renewal projects are a city's genuine attitude towards humanities and history. The current reality is that the performance system of the regional policy determines the ultimate fate of many cultural facilities, but the assessment system is not linked to the culture values on a practical level. The transformation of Dacheng Flour Factory has a good reputation, but it still failed. The core reason is that the city ignores the cultural value brought by such heterogeneity. If we aim to continue the particularity of Dacheng Flour Factory and maintain its cultural value, it requires higher wisdom, improved system, and more patient cultivation.

REVISIT

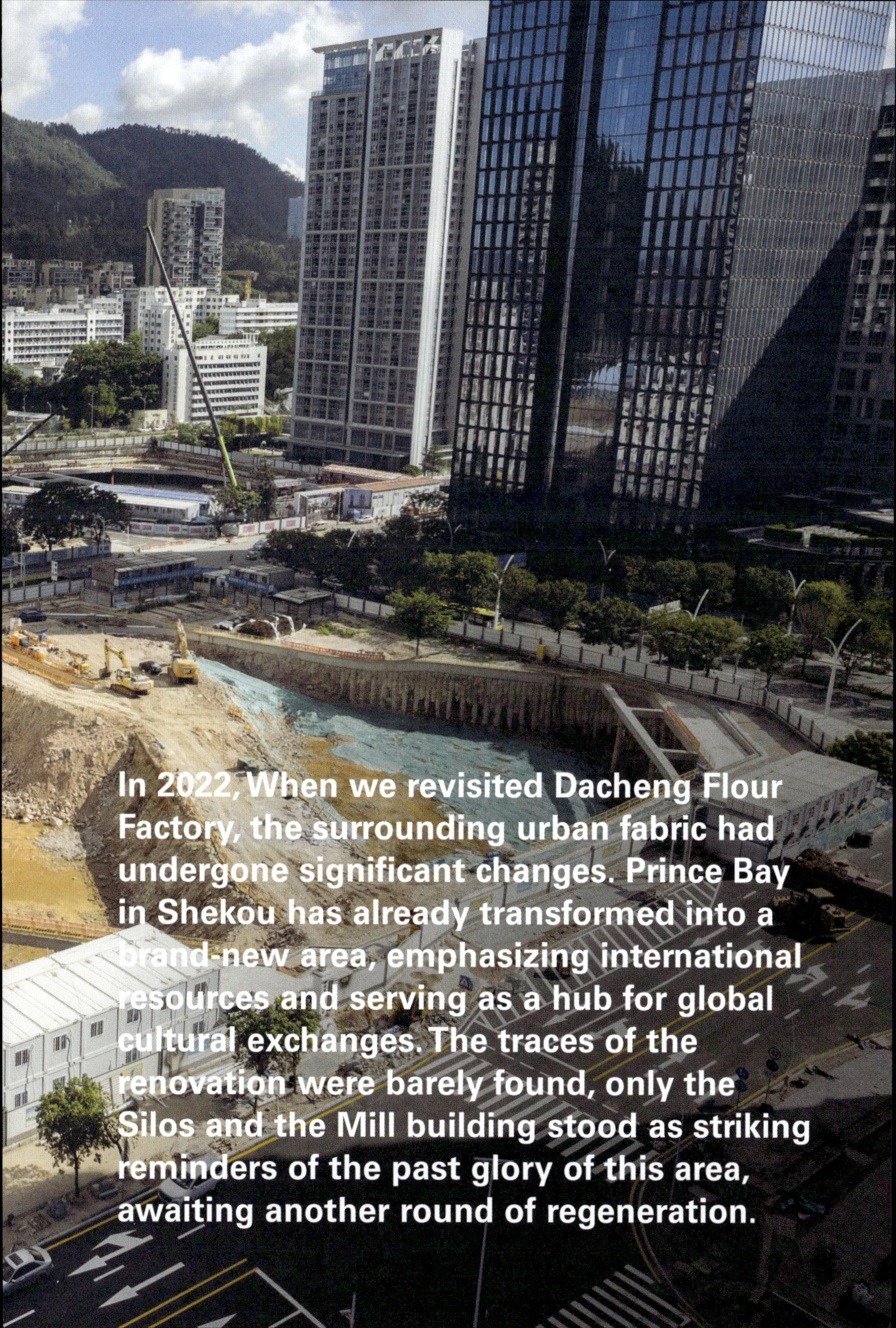

In 2022, When we revisited Dacheng Flour Factory, the surrounding urban fabric had undergone significant changes. Prince Bay in Shekou has already transformed into a brand-new area, emphasizing international resources and serving as a hub for global cultural exchanges. The traces of the renovation were barely found, only the Silos and the Mill building stood as striking reminders of the past glory of this area, awaiting another round of regeneration.

大成麵粉

VIKING

THE UNFINISHED JOURNEY

It has been nine years since the 2015 Bi-City Biennale of Urbanism\ Architecture (Shenzhen), "Re-Living the City." As this book prepares for publication in 2024, Dacheng Flour Factory is embarking on a new chapter. Commissioned by China International Marine Containers Group and designed by Aedas, the construction on the ruins of the former Dacheng Flour Factory is nearing completion, and the new Dacheng Plaza at Prince Bay is expected to officially open by the end of 2024.

The overall spatial development of Prince Bay is also rapidly saturating, just as it was planned years ago. Looking back at the radical and forward-thinking spatial experiments we conducted in terms of preservation, renovation, and renewal at the factory, the current situation is completely different, leaving us with a deep sense of nostalgia – we can no longer return to the starting point and "re-live" it. While not every UABB venue, like OCT-Loft and Nantou Old Town, has seen continuous retention and development, most of the renovated sites either return to their original state or become ruins again. The reasons behind this are complex and cannot be fully explained by a single book or a case study, but the experience and lessons learned from Dacheng Flour Factory are indeed representative. Retelling the stroy of its journey and reflecting on our experience is the key reasons why I hope to compile this book after so many years.

As the architectural team responsible for the renovation at the time, NODE Architecture & Urbanism's detailed documentation of the design and renovation process of the Dacheng Flour Factory makes up the major portion of this book. The images provided by the UABB office allow us to visually revisit the temporary yet experimental and idealistic exhibition site from that period. In addition, interviews with several key participants and decision-makers from that time have been incorporated, including HUANG Weidong, ZHANG Yuxing, ZHENG Yulong, and an interview with myself conducted by ZHONG Gang and *ARTDBL*. I would like to thank the contributors for offering a more objective and comprehensive understanding of the spatial transformation and surrounding development from different perspectives.

Here I would like to express special thanks to my colleague, LIU Si, who served as the project manager of UABB in 2015, for her unwavering commitment and high standards, which have been crucial to this research and publication project, as well as to the editor, XIAO Caizi, for her meticulous attention to detail. Without their dedication throughout the entire process, this book would have been nearly impossible to publish. I'd also like to extend my gratitude to UABB Office, *Domus China* and OMA for granting permission to use the relevant images and texts; to the publisher Actar for endorsing the selection of the post-UABB topic of Dacheng Flour Factory for publication; to Shenzhen University and the School of Architecture and Urban Planning for the financial support; and to my colleagues at the Greater Bay Area Innovation Design Lab for their consistent efforts.

The publication of this book at this point in time is a reckoning of our past efforts. While there are regrets, it none-theless leaves a record of a specific period in the atypical journey of Dacheng Flour Factory.

Doreen Heng LIU
Shenzhen, China
October 2024

2024

大成艺术中心
98 5551
40

ABOUT

Doreen Heng LIU
Author

Doreen Heng LIU is the founder and principal of NODE Architecture & Urbanism (NODE). She is a Royal Institute of British Architects (RIBA) Chartered Architect, holds a Doctor of Design degree from Harvard University, and is recognized as a Shenzhen Special Economic Zone Master of Engineering Survey and Design. LIU and her studio NODE have been engaging in diversified architectural and urban design practices in the PRD and wider region for years. She has taught at the Chinese University of Hong Kong, ETH Zurich and the University of California, Berkeley. Since September 2020, she has been appointed as a Distinguished Professor at the School of Architecture and Urban Planning of Shenzhen University, and Director of the Greater Bay Area Innovation Design Lab.

LIU Si
Director of Publication

LIU Si is currently the Managing Director of the Greater Bay Area Innovation Design Lab at Shenzhen University. With a diverse educational background of architecture, art and business management, she has worked as project manager for the curatorial team of the 6th Bi-City Biennale of Urbanism\Architecture (Shenzhen) in 2015. During that period, she also worked in parallel with the architect team on the renovation of Dacheng Flour

Factory. Throughout her career, LIU Si has been actively engaged in numerous architecture and art exhibition projects, committing to interdisciplinary spatial practices in various capacities.

Shenzhen University – The Greater Bay Area Innovation and Design Lab (GBA Lab)
Research Team

GBA Lab is a pioneer in spatial research and design for the current Greater Bay Area and for global urbanization. Founded by Dr. Doreen Heng LIU, Director/Academic Chair of the GBA Lab and Distinguished Professor at the School of Architecture and Urban Planning of Shenzhen University, the lab explores spatial innovation and various solutions that are responses to front-line issues through cross-boundary and interdisciplinary approaches with design-oriented research methodology, combining experimental design practices, teaching, exhibitions, publications, and academic conferences. It aims to become an engine that powers the sustainable development of architecture.

NODE Architecture & Urbanism (NODE)
Architecture, Urban Design & Landscape
Design Team of Dacheng Flour Factory Renovation Project

NODE was established in 2004. As one of the most influential independent architectural design firms in South China, it has received extensive attention at home and abroad. Founded and led by Principal Architect, Doreen Heng LIU, NODE currently consists of about 20 architects and designers.

Based in Shenzhen and Hong Kong, NODE has long focused on urban space and public life, insisting on ontological research and practice, pursuing innovation based on the foundations of pragmatism, and exploring architectural concepts' inherent logic in relation to openness and compatibility. Through interdisciplinary interaction and stimulation, the studio maintains its forward-looking and experimental nature in architectural design practice.

NODE & GBA Lab, 2024

CREDITS & COLOPHON

Renovation of Dacheng Flour Factory
2015 UABB Venue Planning & Architectural Design

PROJECT CREDITS

Design Period
2015.03-2015.07

Completion Time
2015.11.20

Site Area
32,321 sqm

Building Area
32,780 sqm

Client
China Merchants Shekou Industrial Zone

Architecture, Urban Design & Landscape
NODE Architecture & Urbanism: Doreen Heng LIU, HUANG Jiebin, GUAN Yutao, SHI Xueyuan, ZHENG Guitang, WANG Rui, LI Yangwenzhao (Intern), ZHANG Yu (Intern)

Urban Design Consultant
Urban-ThinkTank: Hubert KLUMPNER & Alfredo BRILLEMBOURG

Construction Documents
Shenzhen General Institute of Architectural Design and Research

Landscape Design of "Floating Fields"
Thomas CHUNG, School of Architecture, Chinese University of Hong Kong

Lighting Design Consultant
Shenzhen Lighting Formula

IMAGE CREDIT

© UABB, Photo by ZHANG Chao, P.2-5
© CHEN Guanhong (ACF), P.6-7

I. HISTORY

© China Merchants Group Shekou Industrial Zone, P.13 (ABOVE)
© China Merchants Group Archives (China Merchants History Museum), P.13 (BELOW)

The Planning Scheme for Prince Bay
© UPDIS, P.46-47, 49
© UPDIS + OMA, P.48

Masterplan of Prince Bay
© OMA, P.50-51

II. WORKSHOP

Before Renovation
© NODE, Photo by ZHANG Chao, P.54-57, 58 (ABOVE), 65, 70-71, 76-77
© UABB, Photo by ZHANG Chao, P.58 (BELOW), 59 (ABOVE), 60-64, 66-69, 72, 74-75
© UABB, Photo by WANG Zhenquan, P.59 (BELOW), 73

International Design Workshop on Creative Development for Dacheng Industrial Heritage Project
© NODE, P.89-90, 93-94
© Archi-Union, P.97-99
© J.MAYER.H and partners, architects, P.101-103
© Office of Ryue Nihsizawa, P.105-106

III. RENOVATION

Construction
© UABB, Photo by FAN Fan, P.110-111
© UABB, Photo by ZHANG Chao, P.112 (ABOVE), 113, 114 (ABOVE), 115 (ABOVE), 116 (ABOVE), 117, 118-119
© NODE, Photo by ZHANG Chao, P.112 (BELOW), 116 (BELOW)
© UABB, Photo by WANG Zhenquan, P.114 (BELOW), 115 (BELOW)

Plan for Shekou's Future: Renovation of Dacheng Flour Factory
All photos, diagrams, drawings and renderings © NODE, P.122-163
except © UABB, P.132, 133 (BELOW), 134 (BELOW), 141 (ABOVE), 143 (ABOVE)
All photos by ZHANG Chao

IV. BIENNALE

During UABB
© NODE, Photo by ZHANG Chao, P.166-167
© UABB, P.168-177

V. OUR FAILURE

Demolishment
© NODE, Photo by ZHANG Chao, P.190-191,192 (ABOVE), 193
© UABB, P.192 (BELOW)
© UABB, Screen shots from video footage by WANG Zhenquan P.194-197

Revisit
© CHEN Guanhong (ACF), P.210-221

The Unfinished Journey
© CHEN Guanhong (ACF), P.223-229

About
© NODE, Photo by ZHANG Chao, P.233

COLOPHON

Published by
Actar Publishers, New York, Barcelona
www.actar.com

Author
Doreen Heng LIU

Director of Publication
LIU Si

Edited by
XIAO Caizi

Graphic Design and Digital Production
Thonik (NL)

With Contributions by

Research Team:
Shenzhen University – The Greater Bay Area Innovation Design Lab (Doreen Heng LIU, LIU Si, XIAO Caizi, LI Sen, YANG Zhiqi)

Interviewees:
Doreen Heng LIU, HUANG Weidong, ZHANG Yuxing, ZHENG Yulong

Associate Editors:
Domus Design Center, ARTDBL

Photography:
ZHANG Chao / WANG Zhenquan / FAN Fan / CHEN Guanhong (ACF) / UABB

Proofreading
Ricardo DEVESA

Printing and Binding
Tiger Printing (Hong Kong)

All rights reserved
© edition: Actar Publishers, editors, Shenzhen University – The Greater Bay Area Innovation Design Lab
© texts: their authors and editors
© design, drawings, illustrations, and photographs: NODE Architecture & Urbanism, Bi-City Biennale of Urbanism\Architecture (Shenzhen), credited photographers

This work is subject to copyright. All rights are reserved, on all or part of the material, specifically translation rights, reprinting, re-use of illustrations, recitation, broadcasting, reproduction on microfilm or other media, and storage in databases. For use of any kind, permission of the copyright owner must be obtained.

Distribution
Actar D, Inc. New York, Barcelona.

New York
440 Park Avenue South, 17th Floor
New York, NY 10016, USA
T +1 2129662207
salesnewyork@actar-d.com

Barcelona
Roca i Batlle 2
08023 Barcelona, Spain
T +34 933 282 183
eurosales@actar-d.com

Indexing
English ISBN: 978-1-63840-114-8
Library of Congress Control Number: 2023948890

Printed in China

Publication date: November 2024

Cover image: © NODE, Photo by ZHANG Chao

Supported by:

ACTAR

ISBN 978-1-63840-114-8 and Library of Congress Control Number (LCCN) 2023948890

The publisher/author/editor has made every effort to contact and acknowledge copyrights of the owners. If there are instances where proper credit is not given, we suggest that the owners of such rights contact the publisher which will make necessary changes in subsequent editions.